Ms. Holmes of Baker Street

The Truth About Sherlock

C. Alan Bradley   William A. S. Sarjeant

Ms. Holmes

of BAKER STREET

The Truth About Sherlock

The University of Alberta Press

Published by

The University of Alberta Press
Ring House 2
Edmonton, Alberta, Canada T6G 2E1

National Library of Canada Cataloguing in Publication

Bradley, C. Alan
   Ms. Holmes of Baker Street : the truth about Sherlock /
C. Alan Bradley, William A.S. Sarjeant. — 2nd ed.

   ISBN 0-88864-415-9

   1. Doyle, Arthur Conan, Sir, 1859-1930—Characters—Sherlock
Holmes. 2. Holmes, Sherlock (Fictitious character)
I. Sarjeant, William A.S. (William Antony Swithin), 1935-
II. Title.

PR4624.B73 2004   823'.8   C2004-901433-1

Printed and bound in Canada by
Houghton Boston Printers, Saskatoon, Saskatchewan.
Second edition, first printing, 2004
All rights reserved.

The University of Alberta Press is committed to protecting our natural environment. As part of our
efforts, this book is printed on New Leaf paper: it contains 100% post-consumer recycled fibres and
is acid- and chlorine-free.

The University of Alberta Press gratefully acknowledges the support received for its publishing
program from The Canada Council for the Arts. The University of Alberta Press also gratefully
acknowledges the financial support of the Government of Canada through the Book Publishing
Industry Development Program (BPIDP) and from the Alberta Foundation for the Arts for its
publishing activities.

To the Creator of Sherlock Holmes
and his special world,

Sir Arthur Conan Doyle.

Contents

Foreword

SEVERAL YEARS AGO the authors put forward the central thesis of this work in a brief paper which appeared in the Sherlockian periodical *From the Mantelpiece*.[1] Our thesis is, to say the least, a controversial interpretation and we were prepared for a barrage of denial, rebuttal and counterclaim. Astonishingly, none came; astonishingly, because Sherlockians, although they are many things, are not silent. And so our cause was bolstered.

When Charles Darwin formulated during the nineteenth century his theory concerning the origin of species, he believed his idea to be an entirely original one. He was astonished and disturbed when he discovered that another scientist, Alfred Russel Wallace, had come to the same conclusions independently. Furthermore, after Darwin had published his great work *On the Origin of Species by Means of Natural Selection* in 1859, it was pointed out to him that the Darwin/Wallace theory had been anticipated several times by other, earlier writers.

We find ourselves in a position comparable to Darwin's. When we first formulated the theory here advanced, we believed ours to be an original inspiration. However, like Darwin, we discovered, even before publishing our hypothesis, that another thinker—in this case, Bruce D. Kennedy—had made the same deductions independently.[2] Again like Darwin, we have learned subsequently of other anticipations of our theory, by Colin Davies[3] and by Esther Sorkin.[4]

However, like Darwin's predecessors, each of these earlier workers stated their thesis only in brief, and without marshalling the volume of evidence necessary to demonstrate the validity of their interpretation. Kennedy, indeed, treated the subject with deplorable levity.

Our own thesis, even if it were not so original as we had believed, was at least presented with somewhat greater care; and, since that time, we have searched diligently for further proofs of our theory.

Subsequent to its publication, a Japanese scholar, Yuro Nakagawa, appears either to have followed it up or to be another who has arrived at the same conclusions.[5] Alas! we cannot read Japanese, but a translation courteously furnished to us by Mr. Katsuo Tamaoka of Hiroshima shows that, even if Mr. Nakagawa's intent is humorous rather than serious, he has independently recognized many of the same lines of evidence that we ourselves have noted. However, we should stress that the translation was arranged too late for Mr. Nakagawa's ideas to have influenced us: nor, though we quote two of his ideas in APPENDIX II, have we borrowed any of our evidence from him.

Throughout the text that follows, the italics in quotations from the Canon are our own, not those of the Chronicler; this applies also in our quotations from earlier commentators (Chapter 2). In the Footnotes, the system of abbreviations originated by Dr. J. Finley Christ, which has since become standard in Sherlockian scholarship, is adhered to when referring to the Canon. It is explained in APPENDIX II, where the published cases are listed in what we are convinced—*pace* earlier scholars—is the correct order. The pagination given in the footnotes refers to W.S. Baring-Gould, ed. *The Annotated Sherlock Holmes.* 2 vols. London: John Murray, 1968. References are cited, for example, as I, p. 125 or II, p. 125, as appropriate.

We present here, then, the results of our literary investigations. Though this is by no means all of the evidence that might be adduced, we believe we have succeeded in accounting for much in the Canon that has been inexplicable hitherto.

Alan Bradley
William A.S. Sarjeant
Saskatoon, Canada; All Hallows Eve, 1987

Acknowledgements

SHERLOCK HOLMES AND DR. WATSON are fictional characters created by Sir Arthur Conan Doyle, and appear in stories and novels by him. Grateful acknowledgement is expressed to Dame Jean Conan Doyle for permission to quote from stories and novels protected by copyright in the United States.

The majority of illustrations herein featured were taken from the issues of *The Strand Magazine* in which Sherlock Holmes's adventures were first revealed to the world. These are considered the most authentic representations of Holmes, Watson and their associates. The illustrations on pages 85 and 101 are by A. Gilbert; those on pages 4 and 97 are by Howard Alcock and that on page 75 by Frank Wiles. All others are the work of Sidney Paget. The remaining illustrations (on pages 27, 91, and 129) are reproduced from G.R. Sims, editor, *Living London*, Cassell, London, 1901.

Linda F. Dietz remained a model of patience and good humour, even though she had to type our manuscript again and again and again as new evidence of Sherlock Holmes's femininity kept surfacing; we are grateful for her labours and for her toleration.

It is a pleasure to acknowledge the wise guidance of Michael Luski, Acquisitions Editor, and project manager with the University of Alberta Press. Lauren Starko's excellent transcription skills eased a daunting task; Alethea Adair, Editorial Assistant, kept mailboxes—both virtual and real—overflowing with work and kindly encouragement. Laraine Coates and Alethea proofed a tricky manuscript with accuracy and aplomb. Cathie Crooks, Sales and Marketing Manager, was a happy presence from day one, while Kevin Zak, who designed both the book and its cover, assured that *Ms. Holmes* would venture forth in her attractive best. And Merrill Distad, Associate Director of Libraries, University of Alberta has been not only an enthusiastic champion of *Ms. Holmes*, but also a comforting and genial friend. Special thanks also to Linda Cameron, Press Director, for making the second debut of *Ms. Holmes* possible.

Alan Bradley expresses his appreciation to all those people who have contributed to his efforts in creating this book. Foremost among them is his mother, Mrs. Ivy Bradley, who provided that kind of home where books were valued and discussed. For friendship, help and encouragement he thanks Michael Harrison, whose works of gentle scholarship remind both authors of the debt we owe to those who worked these same fields before us. Finally, he acknowledges the interest and ideas of his wife Shirley F.A. Bradley, whose patience, love and understanding goes on making it all worthwhile.

William Sarjeant acknowledges equally gratefully the help and the enthusiasm of many friends over the years during which this work was in preparation. The fashion in which his wife, A. Margaret Sarjeant, has shown an affectionate toleration of all the disadvantages of living among a plethora of books, with a husband who spends too much time writing in his study instead of being decently social, deserves and receives his high praise. The help received from other Sherlockians—in particular his fellow Practical But Limited Geologist, Peter Blau of Washington D.C.; Cameron Hollyer, Curator of the Arthur Conan Doyle Collection, Metropolitan Toronto Library; Kate and Christopher Redmond of the Bootmakers of Toronto; and John Bennett Shaw of Albuquerque, New Mexico, greatest of Sherlockian collectors—has immeasurably helped toward the completion of the researches herein set forth.

Introduction

IT IS DIFFICULT TO THINK OF ANOTHER CHARACTER IN FICTION as instantly recognizable, in almost any corner of the globe, as Sherlock Holmes. Certainly there are others who have achieved lasting fame: Gulliver, Robinson Crusoe, and Hamlet all spring to mind, yet they depend on outside factors to make them readily identifiable. Take away the Lilliputians, or the footprint, and Gulliver and Crusoe are simply oddly dressed men, while Hamlet without the skull is just a man in black talking to himself. Sherlock Holmes, however, has insinuated himself into the public consciousness so skillfully that even his trappings identify him for all and sundry. A deerstalker, magnifying glass, or curved pipe—taken singly or in combination—announce his presence, even if the man himself is nowhere to be seen; so much so that these icons are now universal shorthand for a detective, recognised even by people who have never read a Holmes story.

However casual most people's acquaintance with Holmes is, there are others who take the detective very seriously indeed. There have been Sherlockians almost since there has been a Sherlock. The term Sherlockian—used to describe those who study the character and his world with a scrutiny usually only afforded to such works as the Bible and Shakespeare's plays—was first coined in 1903,[1] a scant twelve years after Holmes exploded into popularity in the pages of *The Strand Magazine*.[2] In 1905 an article appeared in *The Monthly Review*,[3] purporting to give the family tree of Sherlock Holmes: his parents are identified as one "Gaboriau Holmes" and "Augustine Dupin (adopted daughter of Mr. Edgar A. Poe, of Richmond, Va.)." From there it was but a short step to Ronald Knox's now famous article "Studies in the Literature of Sherlock Holmes,"[4] first made public in 1911, and generally acknowledged as the genesis of serious Sherlockian study.

Before long, others had discovered the delights of "playing the game," and articles, essays, and books about Sherlock Holmes poured forth with the force of the Reichenbach Falls in flood. No aspect of the Holmes Canon was too large (or too small) to be studied. Battles were fought over the chronology of the stories; the location of Watson's wound; Holmes's travels during the "great hiatus"; how many times Watson was married (and who those women were); the "real" identities of Irene Adler, the King of Bohemia, and the mysterious gentleman known as the Illustrious Client. Biographies were written of Holmes and Watson; train schedules, calendars, and cycles of the moon were analysed, in attempts to date this or that case; the geography of Baker Street was studied with the meticulousness of archaeologists uncovering the ruins of Nineveh or Nimrud, in an attempt to discover where precisely 221B had been located.

Much—if not most—of this scholarship was carried out for the sheer pleasure it afforded; yet on occasion a wave of controversy would break through the placid surface of Sherlockian studies. In 1941 Rex Stout unleashed a bombshell in the form of an article entitled "Watson Was a Woman,"[5] the central argument of which is obvious, while in 1962 William S. Baring-Gould, only slightly less controversially, suggested that Stout's own creation, Nero Wolfe, was no less than the child of Sherlock Holmes and Irene Adler, she of "dubious and questionable memory."[6] These theories, however scandalous they may have appeared to some people, were eventually taken in stride, for Sherlockians are nothing if not broad-minded—just as well perhaps—when the object of one's admiration has been hijacked by everyone from Madison Avenue to cartoonists, from pornographers (on film and in print) to the creators of a popular TV show for children starring a small, talkative dog.

All of which brings us to the book that you are now holding in your hand, and which began life as an article in *From the Mantelpiece* in 1979. Although the authors do not mention Ronald Knox, they clearly took to heart his dictum that "If anyone objects, that the study of Holmes literature is unworthy of scholarly attention, I might content myself with replying that to the scholarly mind anything is worthy of study, if that study be thorough and systematic." *Ms. Holmes of Baker Street* is as thorough and systematic a study of the Holmes

Canon as anyone could wish for; and while some people may disagree with its central thesis, it is impossible not to recognize the precision with which the authors marshal their facts and the skill with which they lay them before the public. In addition to placing the sixty tales of the Holmes Canon into chronological order, the authors have explored several questions that have vexed generations of Sherlockians. Why *did* Sherlock Holmes refuse a knighthood? Why does the detective react so violently towards the scoundrel who has imposed so cruelly on poor Mary Sutherland? How does a man whose knowledge of literature is described as nil come to quote from a letter written by Gustave Flaubert to George Sand, that well known male impersonator? Was Irene Adler's sly "Good night, Mr Sherlock Holmes" meant as a taunt, or as a compliment from one successfully disguised woman to another? And is the explanation for Holmes's three year "hiatus" following the incident at the Reichenbach Falls very different to the one accepted by most Sherlockians?

Ms. Holmes of Baker Street is a radical departure from conventional Canonical studies; but it is one undertaken with the scholarship, wit, and understanding which are hallmarks of the best writings about the great detective and his world. It will give readers something to ponder the next time they pick up one of Holmes's adventures; and one cannot help but think that Sherlock himself would approve of the way in which the authors have argued their case. "You know my methods, Watson; apply them," said Holmes. Alan Bradley and William Sarjeant clearly knew those methods well; how accurately they have applied them, I leave for the reader to decide.

Barbara Roden
February 2004

Notes

1   *The Bookman*, February, 1903. Perhaps fittingly, the term "Sherlockian" was used by the editors to describe a woman, Miss Carolyn Wells.
2   Although Sherlock Holmes first appeared in 1887, in the novel *A Study in Scarlet* (a second novel, *The Sign of the Four*, appeared in 1890), the character did not achieve the immense popularity that is today taken for granted until the short stories began appearing in *The Strand Magazine* in July 1891.
3   R. Bostoun Cromer, [pseudonym of Dorothy K. Broster and M. Croom Brown] "The Questionable Parentage of Basil Grant," in *The Monthly Review*, July, 1905.
4   Ronald Knox, "Studies in Sherlock Holmes" in *Essays in Satire*. (London: Sheed & Ward, 1928).
5   Rex Stout, "Watson Was a Woman," *Saturday Review of Literature*, 23, no.19. (1941).
6   William S. Baring-Gould, *Sherlock Holmes of Baker Street: A Life of The World's First Consulting Detective*. (New York: Clarkson N. Potter, 1962).

The Thesis Presented

THERE IS SOMETHING VERY STRANGE about Sherlock Holmes. Writer after writer has noticed this fact and then, with scarcely more than a shrug, has passed on to other matters. The Sherlockian scholar D. Martin Dakin, for instance, perceived that there was about Holmes "some enigmatic secret in his life to which even Watson never penetrated"[1]—a secret, noted Dakin, that drove Holmes to retire when less than fifty years old and at the very height of his powers.[2] Sadly, Dakin neglected (or chose not) to follow his facts through to the proper conclusion. The distinguished mystery writer Rex Stout also detected this strangeness. However, he misinterpreted the evidence and came to the erroneous conclusion that Watson was a woman.[3]

To the best of our knowledge, only three earlier commentators and the present writers have perceived the truth. Each of us was unaware of the others' work, and each must have experienced the same shock of revelation, the same initial incredulity, and then the same realization that fact after fact in the Canon supported the conclusion that had been arrived at so unexpectedly.

Sherlock Holmes told Dr. Watson repeatedly, in words that varied little over the years: "You know my methods. Apply them."[4] Having followed this precept ourselves, we are now able to state without equivocation that, although Watson was no woman, Sherlock Holmes was.

Why then did Dr. Watson never report this fact? The reason was that, in the beginning, he was himself completely taken in by Holmes's disguise, and because later—well, later was too late! The Victorian world would have made mockery of any woman who posed as a man, especially when she had been following a profession like Sherlock's.

Holmes delighted in walking the tightrope of his deception; time and again, through Watson, we are told the truth. To quote a few examples:

> "...I never mixed much with the men of my year."[5]
>
> "You know my methods in such cases, Watson. I put myself in the *man's* place."[6]
>
> "My life is spent in one long effort to escape from the commonplaces of existence."[7]

We may note that Miss Irene Adler is referred to as "a lovely woman, with a face that a *man* might die for."[8]

A more subtle example is when Holmes asserted that "Man...has lost all enterprise and originality."[9] While this would seem a commonplace enough pronouncement today, it would have seemed odd indeed to Victorian ears. At that time it would have been normal to speak, not of "man," but of "mankind." Holmes, of course, was suggesting obliquely that women continued to be endowed with those qualities.

A much broader hint was given when Holmes asserted benignly:

> "I trust that age does not wither, nor custom stale, my infinite variety."[10]

Yet perhaps Watson was not familiar enough with Shakespeare to recognize this as an amended quotation of a description of Cleopatra—and certainly he did not perceive its implications! Watson cites instance upon instance of Holmes's feminine behaviour and qualities without perceiving their significance. Why, at their very first meeting Holmes said something extremely revealing:

> "Let me see—what are my other shortcomings. I get in the dumps at times, and don't open my mouth for days on end. You must not think I am sulky when I do that. Just let me alone, and I'll soon be right."[11]

Neither then nor later did Watson realize that Holmes was handing him the lock with one hand and the key with the other.

Watson was to be observing such occasions soon enough:

> "...now and again a reaction would seize him, and for days on end he
> would lie upon the sofa in the sitting-room, hardly uttering a word or
> moving a muscle from morning till night."[12]

Yet, despite his medical training, Watson quite failed to perceive the
significance of these periodic indispositions, which were probably of abnormal
intensity. Did not Holmes record, during student days, having been always
"moping in my rooms"?[13]

Perhaps Holmes's recourse to drugs was an attempt to ameliorate these
regular periods of physical distress, and perhaps Holmes's eventual dropping
of the drug habit was because, with increasing age, they had ceased to be
troublesome. Among others, Ian McQueen has noted Holmes's sharp decline
after the Return.[14] Since he did not recognize that Holmes was a woman,
McQueen was not able to attribute it to its real cause—menopause. Holmes
was about fifty by that time.

In the chapters that follow, we will be bringing forward many evidences
of Holmes's femininity which might equally well be regarded as indications of
homosexual proclivities. That alternative can, we feel, be disregarded in
view of the evidences presented (above and later), not only that Holmes suffered
from the physical vicissitudes to which all women are subject until released from
them by menopause, but also twice became pregnant.

However, should internal evidence be demanded, it is proper to consider the
two adventures in which Holmes has dealings with homosexuals—the one a
client, the other an informant. In the first instance, though Holmes perceived
the truth about his client, he was careful to conceal it from Watson (see p. 62–
63). In the second, Watson perceived it also and showed extreme distaste, while
Holmes's comments display a quite reprehensible lack of sensitivity (see p. 98).
These two instances demonstrate that both of them were wholly out of
sympathy with homosexual behaviour, too much so to have ever been involved
in it themselves.

Consequently we do not propose again to consider this alternative hypothesis,
so entirely is it in conflict with all other evidence, whether quoted in these pages
or left unquoted.

Instead, before launching upon our detailed analysis, we will cite a few of the
many direct indications of Holmes's femininity—for example, a knowledge of
perfumes that was remarkable:

Sherlock's confrontations with Steve Dixey, the Negro boxer, which caused the detective—rather deplorably, perhaps—to reach for the scent bottle. (The Three Gables)

"…I held [the paper] within a few inches of my eyes and was conscious of a faint smell of the scent known as white jessamine. There are seventy-five perfumes, which it is very necessary that a criminal expert should be able to distinguish from each other, and cases have more than once within my own experience depended upon their prompt recognition."[15]

Few males retain beyond adolescence enough of a sense of smell to be capable of such refined olfactory discrimination!

We must also recall Holmes's response to the Negro boxer Steve Dixey, in that curious exchange:

"Lookin' for your gun, Masser Holmes?"
"No; for my scent bottle, Steve."[16]

The insult has a feminine quality; and who ever heard of a Victorian gentleman carrying a scent bottle?

Watson, ever candid but ever impercipient, had noted a third evidence, without recognizing it for what it was:

More than once, during the years that I lived with him in Baker Street, I had observed that a small vanity underlay my friend's quiet and didactic manner.[17]

Moreover, when Watson told Holmes:

"You have brought detection as near an exact science as it can ever be brought in this world."[18]

he noted that Holmes

...flushed up with pleasure at my words, and the earnest way in which I uttered them. I had already observed that he was as sensitive to flattery on the score of his art as any girl can be of her beauty.[19]

The attribute of vanity—and indeed, the very word—were more associated with femininity then than today. Moreover, in general, Victorian males seem to have been singularly unobservant—even more so than their counterparts today and in contrast with most females of that day and this. When Holmes remarked to Watson that:

"Observation with me is second nature"[20]

the words "as it is with any woman" might properly have been added.
Holmes's comment that:

"Three days of absolute fast does not improve one's beauty, Watson."[21]

would sound a little strangely from a Victorian male, in whom Holmes's "extraordinary delicacy of touch,"[22] "curious gifts of instinct,"[23] and "almost hypnotic power of soothing"[24] would have seemed quite out of place.

We recognize that these are but straws, not definite evidences; but all point in the same direction.

In an individual so avowedly cold and scientific in his approach to detection, it is surely remarkable that Holmes could say, "I value a woman's instinct."[25] We believe that it is not so much the instinct of women in general, but a personal instinct in particular, that Holmes was rating so highly!

We may note that Holmes "had a cat-like love of personal cleanliness,"[26] "an abnormally acute set of senses,"[27] and "affected a certain quiet primness of dress."[28] All can be taken equally well, either as hints of femininity or as precautions to conceal that femininity.

We wonder also whether Holmes was being facetious or regretful when lamenting:

"Watson, you have never yet recognized my merits as a housekeeper"?[29]

The authors recognize fully that, in making our interpretations of these remarks and these attributes and, indeed, at many other points in the analysis that follows, we risk offending our feminine readership by making generalizations about women that certainly do not apply to the whole range of womankind. However, we live in an age when divergence from the sexual stereotypes is more usual, and much more permissible, than it was during the Victorian and Edwardian times that were the setting for Holmes's investigations. We urge our readers to remember how much more closely the women of Holmes's day were forced, by social circumstances and pressures, to conform to the expectations, not only of their menfolk but also of their mothers, sisters, aunts and peers. Such generalizations are not only easier to make about women of that time than about women of today but also, we sincerely believe, much more likely to be valid.

Similar pressures were, of course, forcing the men of that time to conform closely to their own, very different, stereotype. The gulf between the sexes was infinitely greater than it is today—and the individuals who, like Holmes, dared to traverse it, were infinitely fewer.

It would be as well to note here that, in order to achieve consistency between our direct quotations from the Canon (the sixty published accounts of Holmes's adventures) and our text, we are obliged to adopt the convention, first employed inadvertently by Dr. Watson, of employing the masculine gender when referring to Holmes.

So Sherlock Holmes wished to be known, and so she was known—even, in the earlier years at least, to the worthy but somewhat obtuse doctor.

Sherlock Holmes:
Glimpses of Childhood and Youth

IN THIS CHAPTER and in Chapters Three to Eleven, we present an analysis which will be easy enough to follow for readers who are familiar with Sherlock Holmes's adventures, as recounted principally by John Watson and conveyed to the public by his medical colleague, Dr. (later Sir) Arthur Conan Doyle. However, it will be less easily followed by those who have not read the Canon. Any reader who is impatient to learn the true story of Sherlock Holmes, or as much of it as can now be reconstructed, is urged to turn immediately to Chapter Twelve.

Though we sympathise with such readers in their impatience, we believe it necessary to present our thesis in detail and in chronological order. This will enable our other readers, better versed in Sherlockian lore, to recognize the full volume and consistency of the evidence for Holmes's femininity.

We begin, therefore, with the references contained in Holmes's earliest cases, to his life before he and Watson came to share those rooms in Baker Street. Thereafter the cases will be examined for relevant evidence in their chronological order.

The Gloria Scott, The Musgrave Ritual, and *A Study in Scarlet*

At the time of their first meeting, Watson listed the accomplishments and the inadequacies of his new friend:

SHERLOCK HOLMES—his limits.... Politics.—Feeble.[1]

One can scarcely feel surprised at this assessment, upon reflecting that Victorian women were without a vote. Instead they were expected by their "keepers" to cultivate proficiency in finer matters, such as music. Holmes, noted Watson, "plays the violin well."[2]

The limited educational opportunities then available to his sex account fully for Holmes's utter ignorance of such subjects as literature, philosophy and astronomy. Although, as Dakin notes correctly, a pretence of ignorance is a common form of vanity,[3] we believe that this ignorance was perfectly genuine. Moreover, having missed an education in those subjects during his childhood years, Holmes concentrated subsequently on the disciplines that related to his chosen profession, gaining that good practical acquaintance with British law, that "immense" mastery of sensational literature, that profound knowledge of chemistry and those smatterings of botany and geology which combined so to puzzle poor Watson. However, except for random reading during periods of relaxation, he made no attempt to fill what he considered to be less important gaps in his knowledge.

Though the universities of Holmes's youth would permit women to attend some lectures, they were not allowed to sit for degrees and, most certainly, they were not provided with accommodation in colleges. It was a striving to compensate for educational inadequacies he considered might handicap him that led Holmes into those first adventures in male attire. He knew himself to be vulnerable and it is not to be wondered at that he "never mixed much with the men of my year."[4]

We may note also Holmes's statement that: "Bar fencing and boxing.... I had few athletic tastes."[5]

Again, a literal truth; Holmes did not state that he was a participant in those sports, only that he had a taste for them (as do many women). As in his detection, however, he was a keen observer!

"Trevor was the only man I knew," Holmes continues, "He was a hearty, full-blooded fellow...the very opposite to me in most respects."[6]

Indeed so! And, of course, the Holmes/Trevor friendship came about only by accident:

"...his bull terrier freezing onto my ankle one morning as I went down to chapel."[7]

As Holmes was to state years later, "Dogs don't make mistakes."[8] His male attire might have deceived his male contemporaries, but not the animal. Of course, mid-Victorian households, ultra-respectable as they were, customarily had dogs destroyed who displayed such unseemly habits. "Gone to heaven" was the colloquial phrase and, as we would expect, Trevor's dog is heard of no more.

Years later, after Watson had warned Holmes that he kept a bull pup,[9] Holmes must have manufactured some excuse to assure the animal's swift removal, for there is no further mention of it. Holmes was never one to take foolish risks.

Yet just how long did Holmes's attire deceive his contemporaries? At a time when the universities were notoriously full of "hearties" and rambunctious practical joking, did Holmes's retiring habits and avoidance of participation in games attract resentment and retaliation? In the course of some romp, was it recognized that he was a woman and was he then sent down? This would account for his having attended university for only two years, and also for the evasiveness with which those years were mentioned. The very question of whether his college was at Oxford or at Cambridge has provoked much argument among Sherlockian scholars.[10]

Furthermore, the resultant disgrace might explain another puzzling feature of the Canon—the suppression of all information concerning his home and his parents. It is likely enough that, disquieted by this early attempt to play the male, Holmes's father and mother followed a course adopted by many other Victorian parents and disowned their daughter.

Though Holmes overcame to some extent this early trauma, he was later to admit that "during my last years at the university there was a good deal of talk there about myself and my methods."[11] That, we can well imagine.

It must have been a memorable sight, this tall, grave Sherlock Holmes moving about the university—there, and yet not wholly there, speaking (when he spoke at all) in a "high, somewhat strident"[12] voice. It might, in fact, have been his voice that gave away the secret to his classmates.

Perhaps the jolt of this recognition caused him to drop the pose for a while until he recovered his nerve—the Montague Street period (see below). Once he resumed that pose, Holmes did so forever—or, at least, for the term of his public life. (We may be sure he dropped it in private on occasion, by choice or otherwise!) The impersonation became, for him, a lifelong art:

"Some touch of the artist wells up within me, and calls insistently for a well-staged performance."[13]

Indeed, so well-staged was his performance, and so potent his belief, that it has withstood the keenest scrutineers for nearly a century.

Reginald Musgrave was, in addition to Victor Trevor, the only contact we know Holmes to have retained from his college days. Their acquaintance was slight and involved no more than their having "drifted into talk"[14] now and again. After Musgrave's departure from college, they cannot have kept up any correspondence in the four years before their acquaintance was renewed, since Musgrave was not even certain that Holmes knew of so major a happening as his father's death.[15] If Holmes did indeed leave college under a cloud, it is likely enough that Reginald Musgrave never heard of the incident.

Sherlock Holmes informed Watson that:

"When I first came up to London I had rooms in Montague Street, just around the corner from the British Museum."[16]

In his book *The London of Sherlock Holmes*, Michael Harrison shows that No. 24 Montague Street, Russell Square, was leased for seven years to a Mrs. Holmes. "It would be stretching coincidence too far," he says, "to assume that Mrs. Holmes was not related in some way to young Mr. Holmes."[17]

Indeed, they were one and the same. Holmes was leasing the premises in the guise of a married woman, either to spare himself embarrassment or perhaps to ward off potential suitors, until the time came that he could make the final transformation.

3

Those Early Days in Baker Street

A Study in Scarlet

WHEN STAMFORD, during his lunch with John H. Watson at the Holborn, first mentioned the acquaintance who, like Watson, was seeking lodgings, he reacted rather dampeningly to Watson's enthusiasm:

> Young Stamford looked rather strangely at me over his wine-glass. "You don't know Sherlock Holmes yet," he said; "Perhaps you would not care for him as a constant companion."[1]

Though Stamford proceeded to list a few of Holmes's peculiarities, none of them quite justifies the reservation inherent in that comment. The worst he seemed able to say of Holmes was that Holmes was "a little too scientific for my tastes" and "not a man that it is easy to draw out."[2] Yet Stamford felt it necessary to add:

> "You mustn't blame me if you don't get on with him…. You proposed this arrangement, so you must not hold me responsible."[3]

This exaggerated defensiveness is hard to understand, when Stamford had so small a stake in the matter. We believe that Stamford—a man who had served as a hospital dresser and must have come to know a great deal about humanity—was sensing the true strangeness of Holmes, without being quite aware what that strangeness was.

If so, he was more percipient than was Watson; or, for that matter, than Holmes's and Watson's landlady, Mrs. Hudson. Yet one must remember that, in Victorian times, a deception of the kind that Holmes was practising was much more unthinkable than it would be today. Mrs. Hudson was doubtless quite unimaginative and would only rarely, if at all, witness acting of any kind. There was no television, there were no films, and she came of a class that would not attend plays. The music halls, though they did feature female and even male impersonators, did not demand outstanding acting talents. If a lodger was presented as a man and wore the clothing of a gentleman, that would be enough for Mrs. Hudson.

Perhaps, to some extent, the same ready acceptance of a declaration of sexual identity, supported by the wearing of the right clothing, would have satisfied Watson. Holmes's figure was certainly not of a noticeably feminine kind:

> In height he was rather over six feet, and so excessively lean that he seemed to be considerably taller. His eyes were sharp and piercing, save during those intervals of torpor to which I have alluded; and his thin, hawk-like nose gave his whole expression an air of alertness and decision. His chin, too, had the prominence and squareness which mark the man of determination. His hands were invariably blotted with ink and stained with chemicals, yet he was possessed of extraordinary delicacy of touch, as I frequently had occasion to observe when I watched him manipulating his fragile philosophical instruments.[4]

No, not a handsome man; nor, for that matter, a beautiful woman. Was it, indeed, an awareness of physical unattractiveness that caused Holmes to despair of marriage and to embark, instead, on a career that would involve lifelong role-playing? Or was it a sheer frustration with the restricted opportunities available to a woman in Victorian times? We can only speculate.

As closely as we can determine from Watson's descriptions, Holmes, seen in profile, bore a remarkable resemblance to the late Dame Edith Sitwell. Such an ambiguous physical appearance would have been a help in the playing of a masculine role. We may point out also that, unlike many thin men, Holmes did not have a noticeable Adam's apple; but then, of course, a woman would not!

Watson began, of course, with the assumption that Sherlock Holmes was a man. Holmes stressed his full name even at the outset, when he referred to that chemical test he had invented, not as "the Holmes test," but as "the Sherlock Holmes test."[5] We may note that, when they moved into their lodgings, Holmes was careful to allow Watson to move in first, bringing in his own possessions separately and later, so that there might be no confusion—and no likelihood of Watson unpacking the wrong suitcase. Holmes was careful also, in their early days in Baker Street, to rise much earlier than Watson did; and no doubt, during the times of those periodic indispositions, Holmes remembered to take particular care to avoid arousing his fellow lodger's suspicions.

Even so, it is surprising that the medically trained Watson took so long—a matter of many years, as we believe—to perceive the truth about Holmes. Yet Watson did sense the strangeness of Holmes, as his attempt to analyze Holmes's areas of knowledge (discussed earlier, p. 8) demonstrates. When he identified Holmes's unusual profession, he was both satisfied and deeply impressed—too much so to continue with any further analysis.

We may note in passing Holmes's determination to interrupt his investigation, even at its height, in order to go to a concert. And whom did he wish to hear? Why, the Austrian violinist Wilhelmine Norman-Neruda (1839–1911), one of the few women in Victorian times to attain those musical heights that were normally to be scaled only by males. Says Holmes:

"Her attack and her bowing are splendid."[6]

Of course, it was natural that Holmes should admire any woman willing to attack—to attack, in particular, any masculine preserve. We may note that Watson was not invited along; it would have been improper that he be witness to Holmes's heroine-worship!

The Resident Patient

As will be noted later (p. 152), we consider this to be an early case on the basis of evidence contained in its first, *Strand Magazine* publication. The elaborate sequence of deductions concerning Watson's thought processes was transferred during book publication to a later case (*The Cardboard Box*[7]). However, it fits much better here, when Watson was still relatively unfamiliar with Holmes's ways, than in that other case. We believe that its inclusion into the account

"We strolled about together." Sherlock, though determinedly masculine in adopting the outside position on the pavement (i.e., sidewalk) and carrying the stick, nevertheless instinctively took Watson's arm. (The Resident Patient)

of the later adventure was an anachronism that resulted from action by some inept editor, not by Watson himself. The fact that Holmes was obviously still remembering Watson's incredulity at the outset of the Study in Scarlet serves to confirm the earlier date.

The unframed portrait of Henry Ward Beecher and framed portrait of General Gordon that hung on the wall at 221B, together with Holmes's comments on them[8] fit, we feel, as well with this earlier adventure as with the later. Already Gordon was the hero of the Taiping Rebellion and would have been feted in the Victorian journals. Had Gordon already died—this happened in 1885, four years before the later adventure—it is likely that his heroic end would have been commented upon by Watson or Holmes. The problem of the lack of any mention, however oblique, of the scandal that tarnished the image of Henry Ward Beecher remains, whichever date is assigned, since that scandal took place in 1874.

Holmes's sequence of deductions is a tour-de-force which does not bear directly on our thesis—though we may suggest that a woman might be more likely to strive to follow a man's thought processes than might another man!

The Speckled Band

As this case opens, we find Holmes standing "fully dressed"[9] at Watson's bedside. Holmes himself had been roused by Mrs. Hudson upon the arrival of "a young lady...in a considerable state of excitement."[10]

Clearly, therefore, Holmes and Watson did not share a bedroom. Had they done so, Watson—or, indeed, any doctor, used as doctors are to awakenings at all hours—would have been roused also. Moreover, it would surely have been ludicrous for Holmes to dress fully before awakening someone who was sleeping in the same room.

Separate bedrooms, then; but even so, the episode remains a curious one, as James E. Holroyd perceived:

> Holmes was fully dressed when he awakened Watson at 7:15 on that morning in April, '83. But if the visit of Miss Stoner was as urgent as he appeared to think, why waste valuable minutes getting into his own clothes before rousing Watson? Why not have slipped on one of his many dressing gowns? Or if Masterly modesty forbade him to appear before a lady so scantily garbed, why not have asked Mrs. Hudson to call the doctor immediately?[11]

Well, we can understand readily enough both Holmes's precaution in dressing before he roused Watson and his reluctance to allow Watson in turn to be roused by Mrs. Hudson, with the danger of Watson charging into Holmes's bedroom before Holmes had dressed. But what followed? Watson says:

> I rapidly threw on my clothes, and was ready in a few minutes to accompany my friend down to the sitting-room.[12]

Holmes, it seems, had no objection to seeing Watson in a state of undress!

And what happened to that sense of urgency about seeing the client? Was it so essential that Watson was there at the beginning of the interview? If so, then their relationship was changing profoundly.

Indeed, their relationship—or Holmes's behaviour, at least—*was* changing. In their earliest days at Baker Street, Watson had described Holmes as a habitual early riser. In this adventure, he says:

> He was a late riser as a rule.[13]

However, it is evident that Holmes was still making a point of rising at a different time from Watson.

In this adventure there is the well-known scene in which Holmes "picked up the steel poker, and with a sudden effort straightened it out again."[14] This, however, is no proof of masculinity. Everyone has heard at one time or another of the mother who, in sudden exertion, is able to lift the automobile under which her child is trapped. Dr. Grimesby Roylott's behaviour had been sufficiently threatening to arouse a similar reaction. If we picture Holmes's eye on his child— or in this case, on Watson!—all becomes clear.

When Watson and Holmes went off to Stoke Moran, they engaged a bedroom and sitting room at the Crown Inn. Only *one* bedroom?—but after all, they did not plan to sleep in that bedroom! Instead they used it merely as an observation point before hastening off to that grim house of the Roylotts.[15] After the snake had been scotched and that other doctor had died, it was morning and time for them to return to London!

The Beryl Coronet

A question of the location of the bedrooms in 221B Baker Street arises at this point. As we have noted already (p. 15), Holmes and Watson did not share a

Sherlock pensively contemplates a woman "in whom the love of a lover" has extinguished "all other loves." (The Beryl Coronet)

bedroom. Nevertheless, they slept on the same floor; Holmes goes upstairs from their sitting-room to his room and so does Watson.[16] These rooms, incidentally, had a direct access downward by two flights of steps to the front door.[17]

However, though so close, Holmes's bedroom was forbidden territory to Watson. He does not consider going to look for Holmes there, even when he has stayed up till midnight and has not known on rising whether Holmes had returned.[18]

At some later, unspecified time in their sharing of the Baker Street lodgings, Holmes's bedroom was on the same floor as their sitting-room; thus, for example, Holmes was able to drag his tin box of mementos of past cases directly from his bedroom into the sitting-room.[19] Evidently Watson had, on returning, moved back into that upper room. Was the lower bedroom still forbidden territory to him, we wonder?

The insistence of Watson's questioning about Holmes's plans[20] is surprising, after Watson had gained so prolonged an awareness of Holmes's independent spirit. It suggests a change, temporary at least, in their relationship. Was another change imminent? After he had brushed off Watson's questions and told Watson not to wait up, why was there a touch of colour in Holmes's cheeks, a twinkle in his eye,[21] before he left 221B on that occasion? As we have noted above, Watson nevertheless waited up till midnight! Could there be some jealousy of Holmes's activities on that "congenial hunt"?[22]

Later, Holmes commented that "there are women in whom the love of a lover extinguishes all other loves."[23] Was he speaking from personal knowledge, we wonder?

The Second Stain

There are several features to note here. One is Holmes's failure to react positively to the "queenly" and "intensely womanly" Lady Hilda Trelawney Hope.[24] However, he recognizes that Watson is attracted—indeed, Watson's description of the lady is positively rhapsodic! In consequence of an evident feminine jealousy, Holmes's response to the lady's emotional appeal is extremely cold. Moreover, after she has left, first of all Holmes comments:

"Now, Watson, the fair sex is your department."[25]

and thereafter proceeds with a ruthless analysis, quite evidently designed to put Watson off her. This fails and, afterwards, Holmes is "in a mood which his friends would call taciturn, and others morose."[26] We believe he was resenting the effect Lady Trelawney Hope had had upon Watson and, in particular, those rhapsodizings over her beauty!

A second point, apparent not only here but also in other adventures, is Holmes's attitude to food. Here he "devoured sandwiches at irregular hours"[27] and elsewhere, his indifference to regular meals—a contrast to Watson's solid Victorian preferences—is equally apparent. While we recognize that some males *are* irregular eaters, this attitude is much more common among females.

Note also, that, when Holmes and Watson are sallying forth, Holmes says:

"Put on your hat, Watson."[28]

What man ever orders another to put on his hat—and what wife ever fails to do so?

The Years Before Watson's Marriage

The Reigate Squires

THE SECOND PARAGRAPH of Watson's account merits full quotation:

On referring to my notes, I see that it was on the 14th of April that I received a telegram from Lyons, which informed me that Holmes was lying ill in the Hotel Dulong. Within twenty-four hours I was in his sick-room, and was relieved to find that there was nothing formidable in his symptoms. His iron constitution, however, had broken down under the strain of an investigation which had extended over two months, during which time he had never worked less than fifteen hours a day, and had more than once, as he assured me, kept to his task for five days at a stretch. The triumphant issue of his labours could not save him from reaction after so terrible an exertion, and at a time when Europe was ringing with his name, and when his room was literally ankle-deep with congratulatory telegrams, I found him a prey to the blackest depression. Even the knowledge that he had succeeded where the police of three countries had failed, and that he had outmanoeuvred at every point the most accomplished swindler in Europe, was insufficient to rouse him from his nervous prostration.[1]

Sherlock in a frequently adopted position, resting on a couch—this time following that distressing episode in France. (The Reigate Squires)

This paragraph can be read at its face value, accepting, as Watson evidently does, that the cause of Holmes's condition was the overwork that Holmes reported. (It is clear that Watson was neither involved in this investigation, nor close to Holmes, during those weeks before his journey to Lyons.)

However, we wonder if there was not a quite different explanation for Holmes's condition. Was not Watson perhaps, with his medical training, subconsciously perceiving the truth about Holmes's physical state? His choice of words would certainly lead us to believe so!

First of all, we should bear in mind that a full six months had elapsed since the affair of *The Second Stain*. We do not doubt that Holmes had indeed been investigating the nefarious doings of Baron Maupertuis, but we believe he had had other motivations also.

Why was Holmes in France, and why was Watson unaware that he was there? Even more so than now, France during the nineteenth century was renowned for its sexual tolerances. Consider the words of Watson and their sequence:

…nothing formidable in his symptoms.

His iron constitution…had broken down….

The triumphant issue of his labours could not save him from reaction after so terrible an exertion....

...I found him prey to the blackest depression.

...his nervous prostration.

We suggest that Holmes had stolen away discreetly to France to give birth to an illegitimate child. Whether that child was born alive and had been expeditiously sent away to a wet-nurse as prelude to adoption, or whether it was still-born, we have not means of deciding, since Watson was clearly not privy to the true facts. Either circumstance could have accounted for Holmes's black depression. That the birth had been normal, even though the exertion had been "terrible," seems evident. It is made more so by the speed of Holmes's recovery. Though unable to be aroused from that condition of nervous prostration when Watson arrived, Holmes was back in Baker Street within a mere three days[2]—a brief convalescence indeed, if Holmes's "illness" had been a product of the utter physical exhaustion from which he claimed to be suffering.

It is worth noting also that Holmes agreed to stay at Reigate only after he had been satisfied that the residence was a bachelor one.[3] Though he might be confident, even in his weakened condition, that he could sustain his pose well enough to deceive a household of men, he did not desire at such a time the more searching scrutiny of feminine eyes.

Who, then, was the father of Holmes's child? We have no means of knowing. Certainly it was not Watson and, of the other masculine associates of Holmes mentioned in earlier adventures, none seems particularly likely—unless Victor Trevor or Reginald Musgrave had re-entered Holmes's life in an entirely new role! However, Watson's accounts of cases during these early years are well spaced in date and Holmes must have had many preoccupations, and many acquaintances, of whom we have never learned.

Towards the end of this adventure, Watson is startled to hear Holmes screaming "Help! Help! Murder!" Holmes is discovered prostrate on the ground with the younger villain clutching his throat and the older twisting one of his arms.[4] Where is the skilful fighter of whom, elsewhere, we have been told? A single young man has succeeded in besting him in a brief fight and has even flattened him! Moreover, that scream of panic accords ill with an image of Holmes as a he-man. Since he knew they were in a neighbouring room, why did he not call "Watson! Colonel Hayter! Help me!"?

This scene fits well with our image of Holmes as a woman in a panic—and, in particular, of a woman whom a recent accouchement had drained of her normal strength and fortitude. Later Holmes complains of the "knocking about"

"Help! Help! Murder!" Where is the skilful fighter of whom we have so often been told? (The Reigate Squires)

Sherlock again resting on a couch and, as so often, enjoying the extra concealment afforded by a dressing-gown. (The Cardboard Box)

he had received. Again, this fits well with our interpretation and ill with the image of Holmes the (self-proclaimed) pugilist of note. Surely even nervous exhaustion would not account for this scene!

The Valley of Fear

This case follows what Watson has described as "a long series of sterile weeks."[5] Indeed, eight months had elapsed since the last chronicled adventure and Holmes, sitting pale-cheeked and with glistening eyes in his dressing-gown.[6] He was surely just suffering from one of the spells Victorians discreetly termed "the vapours."

Nevertheless, and even after eight years of sharing lodgings with Holmes, Watson remained unaware that Holmes was a woman. During this adventure, Holmes continued to play that teasing game of words, half telling the truth to Watson, half encouraging him in false assumptions. Holmes states:

"I am not a whole-souled admirer of womankind."[7]

True enough, when he had adopted a male role instead of acknowledging his femininity! See also how Holmes is generating false inferences, without telling any untruth when he says:

"Should I ever marry, Watson, I should hope to inspire my wife with some feeling...."[8]

However, Holmes is speaking the whole truth when he states:

"Some touch of the artist wells up within me, and calls insistently for a well-staged performance."[9]

Whilst in Birlstone, Sussex, Holmes and Watson stay overnight in an inn:

It was late that night when Holmes returned from his solitary excursions. We slept in a double-bedded room, which was the best that the little country inn could do for us. I was already asleep when I was partly awakened by his entrance.

"Well, Holmes," I murmured, "have you found out anything?"

He stood beside me in silence, his candle in his hand. Then the tall, lean figure inclined towards me.

"I say, Watson," he whispered, "would you be afraid to sleep in the same room as a lunatic, a man with softening of the brain, an idiot whose mind has lost its grip?"

"Not in the least," I answered in astonishment.

"Ah, that's lucky," he said; and not another word would he utter that night.[10]

This was the first occasion, on which, so far as we are told, the two have shared a room overnight—and quite evidently Holmes had sought to avoid this, being frustrated by the inadequacies of the inn. His "solitary excursion" was no doubt designed to allow Watson to go safely to sleep before Holmes went to that double bed. His silence, in annoyance that Watson was still awake accounting for that silence, although other explanations are of course possible. Holmes's curious conversational gambit may have been designed to induce disquiet and a request from Watson that he seek other quarters—or a seeking of other quarters by Watson! It failed; Watson was astonished but undaunted; and, after that brief, dismissive comment, Holmes fell again silent.

What happened next? Did Holmes undress and join Watson in that double bed? Did Holmes join Watson without undressing? Or did he stay up all night? We shall never know; but we may be sure that Watson awoke next morning without having learned Holmes's secret!

Certainly, that next evening, Holmes was in a mood of such irritability as to suggest he had a short or sleepless night. The unfortunate Inspector MacDonald bore the brunt of this. During their "long and bitter vigil," he asked innocently:

"How long is this to last?"

"I have no more notion than you how long it is to last," Holmes answered with some asperity. "If criminals would always schedule their movements like railway trains, it would certainly be more convenient for all of us."[11]

The Yellow Face

At first glance, an early statement of Watson's appears to present us with a major difficulty for our thesis. He comments:

Sherlock Holmes was a man who seldom took exercise for exercise's sake. Few men were capable of greater muscular effort, and he was undoubtedly one of the finest boxers of his weight that I have ever seen....[12]

We may discard the problem of Holmes being twice described as a man, on the basis that Watson still sincerely believed him to be so. But the boxing? Yet Watson gives no details to support his asseveration. Did he see Holmes in any actual contests? It seems unlikely; the Canon mentions no such incidents and, in view of Watson's own initial statement, it is highly improbable that Holmes ever sparred for exercise! In the cases which end with a violent encounter with a criminal, there is usually a hand-to-hand scrap that would give no opportunity for a display of boxing skills—and a scrap, moreover, in which Holmes plays no prominent part.

We advance the hypothesis that Watson was merely taking Holmes's own word for those skills and was supplying an unconsciously false testimony here. We recall, on the one hand, Holmes's almost consistently unimpressive performances in the combats that Watson actually witnessed and, on the other, Holmes's glowing accounts of the skill he displayed in encounters—were they actually combats?—when Watson was not present. In absence of any supporting testimony whatsoever, we must simply discount Watson's claim.

Sherlock, if indeed taking part in sparring matches, need not have revealed her femininity, as the garb in this contemporary sporting photograph demonstrates.

We note with interest, however, Watson's subsequent observations. First, that Holmes:

> ...seldom bestirred himself save where there was some professional object to be served. Then he was absolutely untiring and indefatigable. That he should have kept himself in training under such circumstances is remarkable, but his diet was usually of the sparest, and his habits were simple to the verge of austerity.[13]

As we noted earlier (p. 19), whilst it cannot be claimed that all males eat regularly and well, it is surely true that irregular and sparse eating is a virtue— or a vice?—more common among women. In our own time, this tendency is dignified with the name "anorexia nervosa." The alternation of lassitude with bursts of energy has also a familiar enough female explanation.

At the end of this case, when Grant Munro receives with affection the little coloured child of his wife's first marriage—though, according to the original *Strand Magazine* account, only after a "long ten minutes"— Watson's approval is patent; indeed, he is deeply touched. Holmes, in contrast, makes no comment whatsoever. All he does is to lead Watson away from the scene.[14]

Can it be that Holmes felt more deeply than Watson, as a woman might, the Victorian prejudice against mixed marriages? Did he feel himself unable to say anything good about Effie Munro's behaviour and her husband's response to it? Was he, in consequence, removing himself discreetly from the scene to avoid embarrassment?

When he requested Watson to murmur "Norbury" into his ear whenever he seemed over-confident of his powers,[15] was Holmes desiring to be reminded, not of a failure in professional astuteness, but of having come so close to that embarrassment? This would solve a problem that has puzzled many commentators. Since Holmes did not truly fail, why should such a whisper be so salutary? We believe we have given the answer.

The Cardboard Box

In Victorian times, smoking was almost exclusively a male pleasure; indeed, the plot of an Italian opera, Ermanno Wolf-Ferrari's *Il Segreto di Susanna* (1909), hinges upon the husband's assumption, on smelling cigarette smoke, that his wife must have had a lover, whereas in fact she was merely a secret smoker! In assuming a man's role, Holmes gained much verisimilitude by his smoking. Indeed, he was to enjoy pipe-smoking so much that the bulldog pipe has come, along with the deerstalker, to symbolize Sherlock.

Yet he was less successful with cigars, it seems; for this is the only case when we know that Holmes actually smoked one.[16] Though we are elsewhere told of his keeping cigars in the coal scuttle,[17] this eccentric storage scarcely suggests the connoisseur! Probably they were kept for clients—or for Watson. Nor does Holmes's expertise in recognizing cigar ashes,[18] to the point of writing a monograph on them,[19] imply a requirement to be regularly smoking them! We believe his flirtation with cigars was brief and unsuccessful.

The Greek Interpreter

Sherlock's elder and only brother, Mycroft, was of course party to his sister's secret—indeed, how could he fail to be?—but seems to have shown his disapproval only through aloofness. However, it should be noted, that, when greeting Sherlock and Dr. Watson, Mycroft made the following neat distinction:

"Come in, Sherlock! Come in, sir."[20]

Not "Come in, gentlemen," as might be expected.

Mycroft was, of course, a founder member of the Diogenes Club, that gathering-place of "the most unsociable and unclubbable men" in London, where talking is permitted only in the Strangers' Room.[21] Sherlock had been there on occasion and had found it "a very soothing atmosphere,"[22] but it is clear that he was not a member. Naturally not; this was a men's club—and the sexual barriers in London's clubland were very rigid. Mycroft would never have risked nominating his sister to it, however convincing her male impersonation: and, had someone else done so, we may be certain that Mycroft would not have allowed the nomination to go through.

Yet, as we shall see, Mycroft retained a sense of responsibility for Sherlock. Indeed, if so austere a man could be said to feel emotion, it is likely that Mycroft—sharing, as he did, so many of Sherlock's mental aptitudes—was fond of his younger sibling. Maybe that is why they retained contact, even after Sherlock's parents had severed any relationship.

We may note that Sherlock had acquired a revolver by the time of this adventure, one small enough to fit into a pocket—and small enough for a woman to handle. Mr. Robert Keith Leavitt, in an article perhaps significantly entitled "Annie Oakley in Baker Street,"[23] has theorized that this was a Webley Metropolitan Police Model, with a $2^{1}/_{2}$" barrel—a view shared by Scott McMillan and Garry James, in their review of the Holmesian arsenal.[24] This was the tiniest of the weapons then available and could, of course, be carried in concealment without need for a holster. We see no reason to question their judgement.

The Sign of Four

As Holmes's affection for Watson deepens over the years, we might logically expect some small display of jealousy to become manifest, and so it does here.

When Mary Morstan takes her leave of the premises at 221B Baker Street after their first meeting, Watson exclaims "What a very attractive woman!"[25]

Holmes, from beneath drooping eyelids—the classic look of a woman hurt—replies languidly—and we have the feeling that languidness was assumed—"Is she? I did not observe."[26] Such a patent lie could not have come easily to the lips of one to whom observation was second nature; it demanded an emotional motivation.

Moreover, Holmes's jealousy is again made apparent by what follows. "It is of the first importance," he warns Watson, "not to allow your judgement to be biased by personal qualities." And, lest Watson miss the point, Holmes goes on:

> "I assure you that the most winning woman I ever knew was hanged for poisoning three little children for their insurance money...."[27]

When Watson protests, Holmes abruptly changes the subject.

Holmes, it seems, has remained unresponsive to Mary Morstan's considerable charms, though perceiving them all too well and being disturbed by that perception. Indeed, it is later made explicit that Sherlock, with his astuteness and particular understanding of Watson, sensed well enough what was to come. See how he responds when the news is broken to him:

> "Well, and there is the end of our little drama." I remarked, after we had sat sometime smoking in silence. "I fear that it may be the last investigation in which I shall have the chance of studying your methods. Miss Morstan has done me the honour to accept me as husband in prospective."
>
> He gave a most dismal groan.
>
> "I feared as much," said he. "Really I cannot congratulate you."
>
> I was a little hurt.
>
> "Have you any reason to be dissatisfied with my choice?" I asked.
>
> "Not at all. I think she is one of the most charming young ladies I ever met and might have been most useful in such work as we have been doing.... But love is an emotional thing, and whatever is emotional is opposed to that true cold reason which I place above all things. I shall never marry myself, lest I bias my judgement."
>
> "I trust," said I, laughing, "that my judgement may survive the ordeal. But you look weary."

"Yes, the reaction is already upon me. I shall be as limp as a rag for a week."[28]

But, one may ask, the reaction to what? To the case—or to Watson's announcement? Surely, to the latter. While they were smoking in silence, Watson had had ample time to study Holmes; but it is only after the announcement that he noticed that Holmes was looking, as he thought, "weary." Watson is sorry for him:

> "The division seems rather unfair," I remarked. "You have done all the work in this business. I get a wife out of it, [Police Inspector Athelney] Jones gets the credit, pray what remains for you?"
>
> "For me," said Sherlock Holmes, "there still remains the cocaine-bottle." And he stretched his long white hand up for it.[29]

That was a pretty swift flight from the exhilaration of the case to the refuge of drugs, was it not? Yes indeed, Watson's announcement had confirmed Sherlock's worst fears; but we do not believe it was this shock that drove Sherlock to the drugs. Rather, we believe this was a gesture of defiance—defiance of the doctor who had been striving to wean his friend from cocaine, but who had now signified that his personal priorities had switched elsewhere.

Notice also that, in between the two exchanges to which we have referred, there was another and a curious one. Watson comments:

> "Strange...how terms of what in another man I should call laziness alternate with your fits of splendid energy and vigour."[30]

[No, the good doctor had still not recognized Sherlock's periods for what they were!]

To which Holmes responds:

> "Yes, there are in me the makings of a very fine loafer, and also of a pretty spry sort of fellow. I often think of those lines of old Goethe:—
> Schade dass die Natur nur *einem* Mensch aus dir schuf,
> Denn zum würdigen Mann war und zum Schelmen der Stoff."[31]

Then, before Watson—whose knowledge of German was probably infinitesimal, has opportunity to ask what the quotation meant, Holmes steers the conversation hastily back onto the recent case!

Had Watson been able to ask, we do not know what English version Holmes might have produced. May we suggest a possible one?

> "Alas, that Nature made only *one* being out of you,
> Yet there was material for a good man and a rogue."

Holmes is normally presumed to have been referring to himself. We are perhaps the first to offer an alternative interpretation—that Holmes was lamenting the fact that there were not two Watsons, one to marry Miss Morstan and the other to stay with him in Baker Street.

The Noble Bachelor

Yet there was time for another adventure with Holmes before the marriage took place. Oddly enough, it chanced to concern another marriage; or rather, two marriages, one abortive and the other, one trusts, successful.

At its beginning, Watson was in no physical case to appear at his best to his fiancée and had discreetly remained indoors all day:

> ...the weather had taken a sudden turn to rain, with high autumnal winds, and the Jezail bullet which I had brought back in one of my limbs as a relic of my Afghan campaign throbbed with dull persistence. With my body on one easy-chair and my legs upon another, I had surrounded myself with a cloud of newspapers until at last, saturated with the news of the day, I tossed them all aside and lay listless....[32]

Here we have a curious and unexpected glimpse of Holmes as the social lion. Inspecting an unopened letter bearing "a huge crest and monogram," he says:

> "This looks like one of those unwelcome social summonses which call upon a man either to be bored or to lie."[33]

Note the exact phraseology—a man might be bored, but would a woman? Whatever his protestations, would Holmes? If so, why did he attend such functions? As a professional detective, he had little need to do so, surely? We never learn more of this social career.

In this adventure, there is an indication of a warmer and more relaxed relationship between Watson and Holmes. Possibly the strain between them, implicitly if not overtly of a sexual nature, had eased, once Holmes had accepted that Watson was certainly leaving to be married.

Moreover, see how successfully Watson teases Holmes. Asked for information concerning Lord St. Simon's marriage, he reads two extracts from the newspapers, one quite lengthy and distinctly precious in tone.[34] When Holmes has yawningly asked "Anything else?," Watson continues stolidly with a third and, as he ends, says casually:

"Those were all the notices which appeared before the disappearance of the bride."
"Before the what?" asked Holmes with a start.
"The vanishing of the lady."
"When did she vanish, then?"
"At the wedding breakfast."
"Indeed. This is more interesting than it promised to be, quite dramatic, in fact."

And, having seen Holmes fall so satisfactorily into his little trap, Watson answers with splendidly ironical humour:

"Yes: it struck me as being a little out of the common."[35]

Yet Holmes also is in cheerful mood. Later in the adventure, it is his turn to tease Inspector Lestrade, when the policeman is trying to display to Holmes his energy and decisiveness:

"I have been at work upon [the case] all day."
"And very wet it seems to have made you," said Holmes, laying his hand upon the arm of the pea-jacket.
"Yes, I have been dragging the Serpentine."
"In heaven's name, what for?"
"In search of the body of Lady St. Simon."
Sherlock Holmes leaned back in his chair and laughed heartily.
"Have you dragged the basin of Trafalgar Square fountain?" he asked.

"Why? What do you mean?"

"Because you have just as good a chance of finding this lady in the one as in the other."[36]

Altogether, this last adventure before Watson's marriage seems one of the cheeriest in the Canon. It ends after Lord St. Simon has huffily exited, with Holmes chaffing Watson, the prospective bridegroom, about his indignation at that exit:

"Ah, Watson," said Holmes, smiling, "perhaps you would not be very gracious either if, after all the trouble of wooing and wedding, you found yourself deprived in an instant of wife and of fortune."[37]

Yet, note the sudden down-turn in Holmes's mood at the chapter's end:

"Draw your chair up and hand me my violin, for the only problem we have still to solve is how to while away these bleak autumnal evenings."[38]

Evidently Holmes was beginning, after all, to dread Watson's imminent departure.

Watson in Wedlock

A Scandal in Bohemia

IN THE FIRST FLUSH OF MARITAL HAPPINESS, Watson sees nothing of Holmes. "My marriage," he notes, "had drifted us away from each other."[1] Indeed it had. Nevertheless, when he happens to hear rumours of his friend's doings, Watson remains very interested. His first return visit to 221B Baker Street is made on impulse, when chance has guided his feet to that thoroughfare. Holmes's initial reaction to Watson's call is cool:

> His manner was not effusive. It seldom was; but he was glad, I think, to see me.[2]

As many a man has discovered, the reaction of a woman to his reappearance after a long absence tends to be ambiguous, at best; she is waiting to discover his reasons for returning, to find out how he will treat her. Typically, the male is under particularly close scrutiny—as was Watson on this occasion:

> "Wedlock suits you," he remarked. "I think, Watson, that you have put on seven and a half pounds since I saw you."
>
> "Seven," I answered.
>
> "Indeed, I should have thought a little more. Just a trifle more, I

fancy, Watson. And in practice again, I observe. You did not tell me that you intended to go into harness."[3]

Do we detect a touch of pique here? Certainly it is worthy of note that, though Holmes warms to Watson in the passages that follow and involves his friend gladly in the developing investigation, he shows no least interest in Watson's new marriage. He does not ask even the most conventional of questions concerning Mrs. Watson—an omission even more significant then than it would be now. In contrast, Holmes is quite gleeful when he points out the inadequacies of the servant whom Mrs. Watson has unwisely hired![4]

The principal protagonist in this case is the versatile and attractive adventuress Irene Adler, henceforth to be known, not only to Holmes and Watson but to all Sherlockians, as *"the* woman."[5] The effusiveness of Holmes's admiration resulted, we believe, only in part from the fact that she had outwitted him. She had gained it, rather, because she had successfully penetrated Holmes's mask of masculinity and yet, having done so, had chosen to reveal her percipience to him in a fashion sufficiently subtle to elude the duller-witted Watson.

Notice how she does this. First of all, having followed Holmes back to 221B, she calls out teasingly:

"Good night, Mister Sherlock Holmes."[6]

Observe the stress here: not "Mr. Holmes," but *"Mister* Sherlock." Holmes is troubled and half-recognizes the voice but, for once, fails to make an identification.

However, when he finds the letter, he perceives how completely his deception has been penetrated. It is addressed to "My Dear Mr. Sherlock Holmes"[7]— an unnecessary floridity, which is again a deliberate teasing. But then Irene Adler—or rather, Mrs. Godfrey Norton—makes her point explicit, at least to the informed reader. After discussing Holmes's impersonations, she writes:

"But, you know, I have been trained as an actress myself. Male costume is nothing new to me. I often take advantage of the freedom it gives."

And we can add, as Holmes evidently did when reading it, the unwritten three further words "as do you"! But, of course, that "myself" was the giveaway to him, as it was to the present writers.

"Male costume is nothing new to me"—or, for that matter, to Sherlock either!
(A Scandal in Bohemia)

No wonder the former Miss Adler earned Holmes's admiration! Had she not successfully attempted the same game as he was playing and had she not out-detected the Master himself?

The Boscombe Valley Mystery

Whatever Holmes's feelings about Mrs. Mary Watson might have been, in the early days of her marriage she appears to have retained a warm regard for him. When her husband is summoned by telegram to Holmes's aid, she encourages him to go, even before John reminds her unnecessarily of the debt they both owe to Holmes.[8]

Or was Mary Watson being as altruistic as it may seem? She was very prompt in suggesting that "young Anstruther" might do Watson's work for him; exactly what work, one wonders? Was there a certain astringency in her voice when she said to her husband:

"…you are always so interested in Mr. Sherlock Holmes's cases."[9]

and was there a certain defensiveness in John Watson's voice when he replied:

"I should be ungrateful if I were not, seeing what I gained through one of them."[10]

The telegram read:

Have you a couple of days to spare? Have just been wired from the West of England in connection with Boscombe Valley tragedy. Shall be glad if you will come with me. Air and scenery perfect. Leave Paddington by the 11:15.[11]

The message is wistful in tone—"Shall be glad if you will come with me"—and quite wasteful in words. It is also curiously phrased. Holmes was still, it seems, in London; so why did his invitation to Boscombe Valley say "Air and scenery perfect"? We have no indication that Holmes had ever before been in the west of England; and, coming from him, it seems an unlikely blandishment. Was there some meaning here, hidden from us and from Mary Watson, but not from John? Or was it simply that Holmes's unease had caused him, first of all, to telegraph rather than visiting the Watson household and, secondly, to be uncertain and clumsy in phrasing the telegram? We incline to the latter view.

Sherlock, for once, visits the Watson ménage *and soon finds the most comfortable chair. Note her crossing of the legs—left over right, the reverse of the masculine norm.*
(The Stockbroker's Clerk)

After Holmes has helped to bolster his role by referring to Watson and himself as "two middle-aged gentlemen,"[12] he reveals again his feminine faculty for critical observation of the male when commenting on Watson's shaving, which he calls "positively slovenly."[13] This is an implicit reproof upon Mrs. Watson, who had not drawn her husband's attention to the tonsorial inadequacies resulting from the ill-positioned mirror!

The Stockbroker's Clerk

Watson's involvement in this adventure follows an interval of three months during which, having purchased a decaying medical practice in the Paddington district, he has been working too hard to find time to see Holmes. He is surprised when Holmes arrives unannounced, just after breakfast-time, and whisks him off to Birmingham on a new adventure. Since Mary Watson is upstairs at the critical moment and since Holmes goes out immediately to await Watson on the doorstep,[14] there is no encounter between Mrs. Watson and Holmes. Though Holmes was apparently persuaded to make occasional social calls to the Watson household,[15] we cannot be sure that Mary was ever present; certainly, no face-to-face encounter between Holmes and Mary is recorded in the Canon after the time of Watson's marriage. As we shall see, Holmes seems to have been adroit in avoiding any such event.

Sherlock commits a social gaffe (for any man) by remaining seated in the presence of a lady (Mrs. St. Clair)—and in that lady's own home! (The Man with the Twisted Lip)

The Man with the Twisted Lip

A problem is presented to Sherlockian scholars early in the case, when the frantic Mrs. Whitney has made her dramatic entrance into the peace of the Watson residence. Perhaps merely to calm her, perhaps with a touch of sarcasm, Mary Watson says to her:

> "It was very sweet of you to come. Now, you must have some wine and water, and sit here comfortably and tell us all about it. Or should you rather that I sent James off to bed?"

But Mrs. Whitney replies:

> "Oh, no, no. I want the doctor's advice and help too."[16]

It has been assumed that Mrs. Watson must here have been referring to her husband; but, as is made clear in many other places, his name was John—John

H. Watson. Many theories have been advanced to explain this. They range from the reasonable—Dorothy Sayers's suggestion that Watson's second name was Hamish and that his wife was merely Anglicising this Gaelic name[17]—to the wild—Giles Playfair's suggestion that John Watson was avoiding a libel action by having his wife refer to him as "James."[18] Weirdest of all is the suggestion that Mary Morstan might have been a spy in the Watson household, and married to one James Moriarty![19] That particular suggestion, we feel, can be dismissed out of hand.

A suggestion which, we consider, comes closer to the truth has been made by A. Carson Simpson—that James was Watson's stepson.[20] However, we cannot accept this since there is no least indication in *The Sign of the Four* even that Mary Morstan had ever been married, let alone that she had borne a son. Nor do we believe that Watson had either been married previously or that he had acquired a son through some extramarital liaison. Instead, we would like to propose a quite different and novel explanation: that Watson, relaxing in his chair while Mary knitted, was keeping his eye on their own newly-born son. Whilst a modern wife might well talk cheerfully of "sending" her husband off to bed, no Victorian wife would have done so. Is it not much more likely that she was proposing to send an infant off to bed, so that it might not distract the adults by sudden, demanding cries? If so, it would be natural enough to expect a doctor husband to take the child away to its room and its nurse, while wife Mary conversed with her guest, and equally natural that the guest should protest:

"No, no, no. I want the doctor's advice…"[21]

The child is never referred to again; nor, for that matter, is there any subsequent reference to "James" Watson. We interpret this to indicate that poor little James, like so many Victorian children, failed to survive his infancy. His early death might have well been a major contributing factor to the deterioration of the relationship between John and Mary Watson.

Indeed, there are indications that the relationship was deteriorating already. Watson notes, most peculiarly, that:

Folk who were in grief came to my wife like birds to a lighthouse.[22]

Misery, like grief, notoriously loves company. Was Mary already unhappy? Or was Watson expressing his own early regret at the marriage? Birds attracted to a

Holmes and Watson travelling by train. Whatever happened to poor Sherlock's right arm? Or was she sitting on someone? (The Naval Treaty)

lighthouse usually collide with its glass and die. A simile more indicative of fatal allure could scarcely be found.

Several commentators have remarked on Holmes's peculiar behaviour during this case.[23] Some of it, at least, can be explained by his understandable coyness when faced with the problem of spending a night in a room in Watson's company. We have noted (p. 25) how he tackled this problem on an earlier occasion. In this instance, Holmes simply refuses to go to bed at the St. Clair residence. He removes only his coat and waistcoat before donning a large blue dressing gown, whose provenance remains unexplained. In the morning, says Watson candidly:

> ...a sudden ejaculation caused me to wake up.
> "Awake, Watson?" [Holmes] asked.
> "Yes."
> "Game for a morning drive?"[24]

Holmes leaves discreetly before Watson dresses. It is evident that they were still not on the terms of intimacy that they were to attain later.

The Naval Treaty

In this adventure there seems, at first sight, to be a demonstration of Holmes's fighting ability. According to his account, when Joseph Harrison came at him with a knife, Holmes "had to grass him twice...before I had the upper hand of him."[25]

However, as so often when Holmes's fighting ability was being vaunted, there was no eyewitness to the episode! All we know for sure is that Holmes suffered an injury from that knife and that Harrison got away. Was he released deliberately, as Holmes claimed, or did he make his own escape?

The Crooked Man

At the beginning of this adventure, Holmes arrives at Watson's house at 11:45 P.M., after Mrs. Watson has gone upstairs and the servants had retired to bed. It is evident that Holmes's late arrival, which is not otherwise explained, was planned deliberately to avoid encountering Mrs. Watson; but in other respects the episode is a very odd one. Sherlock asks:

> "Could you put me up to-night?"
> "With pleasure."
> "You told me that you had bachelor quarters for one, and I see that you have no gentleman visitor at present. Your hatstand proclaims as much."
> "I shall be delighted if you will stay."
> "Thank you. I'll fill a vacant peg, then."[26]

Abandoning with reluctance the picture of Holmes hanging from a hat-peg, let us consider what happens later. Yes, Holmes—who has asked no questions and made no remark about Mary Watson—does stay overnight. Yet why does he choose to do so, only to rise so late the next day that he and Watson do not arrive at the scene of the tragedy until midday? Could he not equally well have come to the Watsons' residence in the morning, if there was so little urgency? Did he stay late a-bed to avoid a meeting with Mrs. Watson? As we have noted earlier (p. 39), in none of the adventures after *The Sign of the Four* is any face-to-face encounter between Sherlock and Mary described. Coincidence?

The Engineer's Thumb

An early sentence in this chronicle is worthy of note. Watson writes:

> I had returned to civil practice, and had finally abandoned Holmes in his Baker Street rooms, although I continually visited him, and occasionally even persuaded him to forgo his Bohemian habits so far as to come and visit us.[27]

"Abandoned," of course, was a much more potent word in Victorian times. It carried a connotation of finality, of leaving someone to their fate—and usually, at that, a close relative or lover. It carried also an undertone of guilt, however slight: Watson was surely aware of Holmes's dismay, even anger, at his departure and felt some qualm of conscience.

And those rare visits to the Watson ménage—was Watson, by using the word "us," referring to Mary and himself—which would counter our suspicion that Holmes was deliberately avoiding her—or was it used merely to refer to the Watson household, whether or not its mistress were present? This is a crucial question; yet all we can do is to reiterate that the chronicles describe no direct encounter between Sherlock and the woman who had supplanted him.

Incidentally, the remarkable phlegm displayed by the unfortunate Mr. Hatherley repays study by all who admire the Englishman's stiff upper lip. After a lengthy journey to Watson's door, he indulges in much polite verbal intercourse before understandably becoming overcome with hysterical merriment and thus reminding the worthy doctor that he is there for medical attention, not just for social chit-chat.[28] Such fortitude commands our admiration.

The Five Orange Pips

During this adventure, Mary Watson is away on a visit to her aunt and John is temporarily back at Baker Street. It begins as a rather trying visit, for Holmes is stated to be moody[29] and, while talking with Openshaw, loses his temper quite violently, shaking "his clenched hands in the air."[30] Later, "Again Holmes raved in the air."[31] Holmes's pride is hurt by the death of his client:

> He sprang from his chair, and paced about the room in uncontrollable agitation, with a flush upon his sallow cheeks, and a nervous clasping and unclasping of his long, thin hands.[32]

Sherlock seen in a rare, revealing rear view. Notice the breadth of the pelvic structure.
(The Five Orange Pips)

Later in the evening he enters:

> …looking pale and worn. He walked up to the sideboard, and, tearing a
> piece from the loaf, he devoured it voraciously, washing it down with
> a long draught of water.[33]

Altogether in this adventure Holmes seems in a very unstable mood. No doubt
it was not the right time of the month in which to endure so emotionally
stressful an adventure!

A Case of Identity

This is the first chronicle in which Holmes's love of jewellery is made
apparent.[34] He takes very evident pride in displaying the snuff-box with the

"great amethyst in the centre of the lid" received from the King[35] —and, be it noted, urging Watson to take snuff without showing any sign of doing so himself! He displays also the "remarkable brilliant" he had received from the reigning family of Holland.[36]

In the Victorian period, a taste for jewellery was not only normal, but to be commended, among women. For a man to wear jewellery, however, was considered to be undesirably ostentatious, typical of foreigners and not of true Englishmen—and therefore, by definition, in poor taste.

Later there is for Holmes that "remarkably fine emerald tie-pin" received from that "certain gracious lady" of Windsor.[37] Was the offer of the knighthood to Holmes truly refused or was it withdrawn hastily, and this gift substituted, upon the urgent solicitation of brother Mycroft?

All in all, this is a remarkable and opulent collection of jewellery for any Victorian man to have owned. However, at a time when women took a particular pride in having large and ostentatious jewels to display, it fits very well with our thesis!

It was during this case that Holmes responded with remarkable anger to the treatment of Miss Mary Sutherland by the bogus "Hosmer Angel"—a more extreme reaction than he had shown to many much more serious crimes. (After all, this was a world that contained Jack the Ripper and other equally savage criminals!) Holmes even comments that "there never was a man who deserved punishment more."[38]

Surely this is comprehensible only if viewed as the reaction of one woman to the plight of another? Is it possible, then, that Holmes himself had endured the pangs of a similar betrayal? Why, certainly he had! Had there not been that hasty journey to France (see p. 22), to rid himself of the illegitimate child?

The Blue Carbuncle

The only point of note in this adventure—apart from Holmes's and Watsons's sedulous mutual avoidance of giving each other Christmas greetings—is a very acute piece of feminine observation by Holmes:

> "This hat has not been brushed for weeks. When I see you, my
> dear Watson, with a week's accumulation of dust upon your hat, and
> when your wife allows you to go out in such a state, I shall fear that you
> also have been unfortunate enough to lose your wife's affection."[39]

Sherlock again on the couch, in a very feminine posture and engaged in demonstrating to Watson her special feminine percipience. (The Blue Carbuncle)

The Copper Beeches

This adventure finds Watson firmly entrenched back at Baker Street. Not only is he breakfasting with Holmes, but also he refers to the fact that "Our gas was lit"[40]—a phrase no visitor would use. On this occasion, it cannot be a mere, brief visit of the sort he has made earlier, when Mary Watson was off to see some aunt or other relative or friend. "Our gas was lit"—those are the words of a resident, of one who was sharing expenses.

It is tempting to suggest that Sherlock had lured John away from his wife by some overt feminine advance; but such an argument does not withstand scrutiny. On the contrary, it is evident that Watson has not yet seen through Holmes's great deception, for he is disappointed when, at the end of the adventure, Holmes shows no further interest in Miss Violet Hunter.[41]

That lack of interest need of course, not surprise us. Unlike Watson, we may perceive that Holmes's favourable impression of Miss Hunter derived, in part at least, from the fact that she was a woman making her own way in the world.

However, it leaves us without any definite explanation of what must surely have been an estrangement between John and Mary. Was it that Mary was becoming increasingly jealous of John's attachment to Sherlock? Did she resent her husband's spending so much time at Baker Street and, when at home, in writing up what Sherlock calls, in his disparagement of them, "those little records of our cases"?[42] Had she perhaps, without being clearly aware of Holmes's femininity, come to sense a particular feminine quality in the relationship between the detective and Watson? We believe so.

Silver Blaze

Watson's residence was either continuing, or had been resumed, at the time of this adventure since, at its end Holmes invites Colonel Ross back "to smoke a cigar in our rooms."[43]

At first reading, Holmes seems to exhibit an unexpected knowledge of the costs of women's clothing:

> "Madame Darbyshire had somewhat expensive tastes," remarked Holmes, glancing down the account. "Twenty-two guineas is rather heavy for a single costume."[44]

However, too much cannot be made of this point, for the sum—at least US$800.00 in modern terms—was large enough to impress even a mere male!

The Red-Headed League

By this case, John Watson's second residence in Baker Street had ended, for he begins his account:

> I had called upon my friend, Mr. Sherlock Holmes, one day in the autumn....[45]

So it seems that the quarrel with Mary had been resolved and John was back at his home in Kensington.

Here, Watson refers to Holmes's "dual nature," commenting that:

> The swing of his nature took him from extreme languor to devouring energy; and, as I knew well, he was never so truly formidable as when, for days on end, he had been lounging in his arm-chair amid his improvisations and his black-letter editions.[46]

It is noteworthy that a woman is often at her most energetic after emerging from her regularly recurrent indispositions.

We may remark also that, whilst Holmes urged Watson to bring along his service revolver when they set off for the bank vaults,[47] he took no similar weapon himself. We know that he could shoot well, for had he not shot Tonga from one moving boat, when the pygmy was in another,[48] and had he not decorated his living room wall with a patriotic VR by means of some similar weapon?[49] There is only one reasonable explanation, we feel: that Holmes, being a woman, by now preferred a man—her man, in desire if not in actuality—to carry the gun!

At the end of this adventure Holmes, who gave little other evidence of a knowledge of the world of literature, quoted from memory Gustave Flaubert's letter to George Sand, perhaps the world's best known male impersonator:

"L'homme est rien—l'oeuvre c'est tout."[50] ["Man is nothing—the task is all."]

Was Holmes again teasing Watson with a double entendre?

"My life," said Holmes, "is spent in one long attempt to escape the commonplaces of existence."[51]

Indeed it was!

The Dying Detective

Watson is here summoned from his home to Baker Street by Mrs. Hudson, his former landlady, who tells him "of the sad condition to which my poor friend [Holmes] was reduced."[52] Having arrived, he is ordered not to come too close[53]—reasonably so, since as a medical man he might well perceive Holmes's condition to be less grave than is being pretended.

Nevertheless this is an interesting situation, for it is the first occasion on which Watson has entered Holmes's bedroom. At the end of the adventure, after the villain has been arrested—by Inspector Morton, be it noted, and not by Holmes—the Inspector and his captive are sent away by cab, Holmes promising to follow.[54] Watson, however, is allowed to remain; to witness Holmes's toilet; and to help Holmes on with his coat. However, it does not seem that Holmes undressed from his sleepwear to dress again in outdoor clothes; thus it must be presumed that, to preserve his modesty—and his secret!—he was lying between the blankets fully clothed.

This becomes perfectly comprehensible when one realizes that Holmes had orchestrated the entire scene. He had sent Mrs. Hudson to the Watson residence, making sure she would tell the right "story."[55] (It is to be noted that the worthy landlady never claimed her visit to be spontaneous.) Consequently, he knew Watson would be coming and was able to be properly prepared. Nevertheless, woman-like, he felt it necessary to account for his haggard appearance—and in the words a woman would use:

> "Three days of absolute fast does not improve one's beauty, Watson."[56]

The whole staged scene is admirably and succinctly explained when Holmes states:

> "That pretence I have carried out with the thoroughness of the true artist."[57]

The Final Problem

> "It may be remembered that after my marriage, and my subsequent start in private practice, the very intimate relations which had existed between Holmes and myself became to some extent modified."[58]

Thus Watson—in a sentence that might allow for several very different interpretations! Watson had, of course, returned to his wife after that second period in Baker Street, but the intervening adventures make little mention of Mary—where was she when that summons came from Mrs. Hudson? One suspects that their marital relationship had never recovered its original closeness.

It is evident also that Holmes still had no desire to meet Mrs. Watson:

> "Is Mrs. Watson in?"
> "She is away upon a visit."
> "Indeed! You are alone?"
> "Quite."
> "Then it makes it the easier for me to propose that you should come away with me for a week on to the Continent."

"Where?"

"Oh, anywhere. It's all the same to me."[59]

Note that Sherlock Holmes does not trouble to inquire as to the duration of Mrs. Watson's absence. Nor does he expect Watson to obtain her agreement to, or even inform her of, his sudden departure!

It is also to be noted that Holmes requests Watson's permission to close the shutters and that, when he departs from the house, he does so unconventionally, by scrambling over the back garden wall.[60] Were these indeed devices to escape the attention of Moriarty's minions, as Holmes claimed, or had they some other purpose? Was it, rather, that he wished to avoid the notice of neighbours who might afterwards report the visit—serving, as it did, as prelude to John's departure Continent-ward—to Mrs. Watson?

Watson remarked upon the fact that Holmes was "looking even paler and thinner than usual." In response to this comment, Holmes admits:

"Yes, I have been using myself up rather too freely.... I have been a little pressed of late."[61]

As we shall strive to demonstrate later, this phrase was another example of Holmes's telling the truth to Watson, yet in such a fashion that the worthy doctor quite failed to perceive its real meaning.

And so, off Watson and Holmes go to the Continent, where Holmes has his adventure at the Reichenbach Falls and vanishes from Watson's ken for three long years. The unhappy Watson, mourning what he believes to be the death of his friend, returns to London and to a medical practice and marriage, neither of which are proving particularly successful. The reasons for Holmes's vanishing, and the vexed question of what happened during what Sherlockians call the Great Hiatus, will be examined in the next chapter.

The Great Hiatus

WHEN SHERLOCK HOLMES had returned to London and had been reunited with Watson, he described his encounter with the evil Professor Moriarty and explained how, when the Professor fell to his death in the tumult of the Reichenbach Falls, he himself contrived to escape. Thereafter he accounted for his lengthy silence in the following terms:

> "Several times during the last thee years I have taken up my pen to write to you, but always I feared lest your affectionate regard for me should tempt you to some indiscretion which would betray my secret.... As to Mycroft, I had to confide in him in order to obtain the money which I needed. The course of events in London did not run so well as I had hoped, for the trial of the Moriarty gang left two of its most dangerous members, my own most vindictive enemies, at liberty. I travelled for two years in Tibet, therefore, and amused myself by visiting Lhassa and spending some days with the head Llama [*sic*]. You may have read of the remarkable explorations of a Norwegian named Sigerson, but I am sure that it never occurred to you that you were receiving news of your friend. I then passed through Persia, looked in at Mecca, and paid a short but interesting visit to the Khalifa at

Khartoum, the results of which I have communicated to the Foreign Office. Returning to France, I spent some months in a research into the coal-tar derivatives, which I conducted in a laboratory at Montpellier, in the south of France. Having concluded this to my satisfaction, and learning that only one of my enemies was now left in London, I was about to return when my movements were hastened by the news of this very remarkable Park Lane Mystery, which not only appealed to me by its own merits, but which seemed to offer some most peculiar personal opportunities. I came over at once to London, threw Mrs. Hudson into violent hysterics, and found that Mycroft had preserved my rooms and my papers exactly as they had been. So it was, my dear Watson, that at two o'clock today I found myself in my old arm-chair in my own old room, and only wishing that I could have seen my old friend Watson in the other chair which he has so often adorned."[1]

A fascinating tale this is, indeed, but patently untrue! So patently, indeed, that it has been the subject of prolonged critical scrutiny by Sherlockian scholars. Jack Tracy comments:

> In the absence of supporting evidence, an enormous number of alternate theories have been formed to account for Holmes's activities during this period, each more outrageous than the others.[2]

Even disregarding the sheer scale and variety of his alleged achievements within so short a time span there are excellent reasons for viewing Holmes's account with doubt. Quite certainly we may reject out of hand all those wild stories about Tibet, Persia, Mecca and Khartoum. Had Holmes indeed been so much out of doors, especially in such hot countries as Iran, Arabia and the Sudan, he might well have been "thinner and keener than of old" but he would certainly have been tanned and fit. Instead, as Watson remarked, "there was a dead-white tinge in his aquiline face" that told Watson "his life recently had not been a healthy one."[3]

Among the many indications of Holmes's lack of veracity is an inaccuracy that D. Martin Dakin has noted:

> Nor could [Holmes] have paid even the shortest visit to the Khalifa at Khartoum, seeing he left there for Omdurman in 1885.[4]

We may also join Dakin in wondering about the language in which Holmes spoke to the "Grand Lama," seeing that Holmes had no knowledge of eastern tongues, whilst the Dalai Lama of that time certainly spoke no English!

It is also worthy of stress that, in the many subsequent accounts of the adventures of the reunited pair, there is never another mention of all those splendid, wild places that Holmes claimed to have visited. Nor do Holmes's later life and attitudes reflect any of the sorts of changes in philosophy and thought that a sojourn in Lhasa or in Mecca might have generated. The whole rigmarole has the same ring of careful elaboration about it as that of a tale told by a tardy and guilt-ridden husband to his justifiably indignant wife—or vice versa.

Of the various adventures which Holmes pretended to have experienced during his absence, the most puzzling is his claim to have been investigating coal-tar derivatives in Montpellier. At no earlier time had he shown a concern with any topic so mundane. Could it be that he was indeed in Montpellier, but for quite other reasons?

Before striving to answer that question, it is well to hark back to the sequence of events prefacing Holmes's disappearance. There was that rapid and furtive arrival at, and departure from, Watson's house. There was Mycroft Holmes's astonishing arousal from indolence to hasten Holmes to his train— and thus, safely out of the country. (We may be sure that this guise as a coach-man was not assumed merely so that he might fetch Watson!) There was the very fact that Holmes found need, in his distress, for the comfortable presence of Watson, at least for a few days longer, when it would surely have been simpler and safer—other things being equal—for him to travel alone. Quite clearly, the vanishing had been orchestrated, if not rehearsed, and Watson was a vitally necessary audience to ensure the success of the show.

Some commentators have carried their doubts further. They have alleged that Holmes's story of the threat from Moriarty was a fabrication, designed to explain this absence.[5] They note that Watson himself never met the sinister Professor, instead merely recording Holmes's accounts of his own encounters. They suggest, indeed, that there never was such a "Napoleon of Crime" in London and that, in Germany, there was no actual menace to Holmes at the Reichenbach Falls.

We do not go along with these arguments. We note, for example, that Moriarty's activities were mentioned by Holmes as early as the affair of *The Valley of Fear*.[6] Furthermore, we believe that Colonel Sebastian Moran was, when endeavouring to shoot Holmes with that remarkable air-gun, striving to eliminate one whom he perceived as a dangerous threat to his own freedom. However, that does not reduce the doubt with which we view the rest of Holmes's chronicle of alleged adventure. Nor does it modify in any way our belief that Holmes utilized the menace from the Professor to further his own particular deceit.

Now, let us be quite clear. If the reasons advanced by Holmes were genuine, they would have explained an absence of days or weeks, while the Moriarty gang was rounded up. Yet soon Moriarty was dead and only two of the gang had escaped the police net—the undoubtedly dangerous Colonel Moran and that mysterious second figure who, having gone abroad, is never afterwards mentioned. (Incidentally, this contradicts Holmes's earlier statement to Watson that, of the whole gang, only one, Moriarty himself, had eluded capture; in Chapter Twelve we will suggest why Moran, at least, was neither arrested nor mentioned by Holmes as having escaped arrest.) Would the courageous and ingenious Sherlock Holmes really, from sheer fear of two men, stay out of England for three whole years? Come now; that is not the Holmes we have learned to love and admire! No; some utterly different explanation must be sought.

The primary evidence is surely to be found in Holmes's physical condition on his return, "thinner and keener" and with that "dead-white tinge" in his face. Quite clearly his experiences had been physically debilitating. Was it an illness, maybe, or some other major physical stress?

We believe the latter. We believe that Holmes left England to conceal the fact that he was again pregnant and to seek some remedy for that condition. This provides an excellent reason why the otherwise indolent Mycroft should exert himself so vigorously to get Sherlock out of England. We have suggested that Holmes had visited France before, for a similar purpose (see p. 22). Moreover, we know that he had cousins in France, the Vernet family; had he sought their aid this time? As we pointed out earlier, during the nineteenth century the French were notoriously more tolerant in such matters than the British. Was an abortion arranged? Or was the baby born, to be nurtured by Holmes and sheltered by those French cousins?

Whatever the outcome, Holmes was hit so hard that, even after three years, the physical effects were still immediately perceptible. Watson, though he was himself recuperating from having "fainted for the first and last time,"[7] noticed them straight away. It must be recalled that Holmes was thirty-seven at the time of his vanishing—an advanced age for a first, or even for a second, pregnancy.

If we have found the true explanation, who was the father? Was it because Holmes was evincing strong interest in some other male friend that Watson

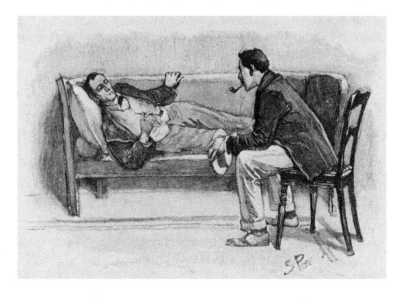

Victor Trevor, the "hearty, full-blooded fellow," visits a couch-bound Sherlock during student days. Was there a later, more intense encounter? (The Gloria Scott)

had returned to his wife? Or might the father have been Watson himself? Was that why Watson accepted Holmes's proposal for the journey to the Continent so unhesitatingly?

Let us first of all dismiss the idea that the father was Watson. Had that been the case, there would have been no need for the elaborate staging of a disappearance: Watson would have known why Holmes was going away, if not whither he was going. Moreover, we cannot believe Watson to be anything other than the staunch and sterling character he has always appeared. He was certainly not one to abandon a woman at the time of her greatest need. No, we are convinced that—even at this late state in their friendship—Watson was still deceived by Holmes's masquerade, still unaware that the detective was a woman.

Who might the father have been, then?

Holmes's old friend Victor Trevor, the only close friend Holmes made during his two years at college,[8] is a serious possibility. Holmes, we may remember, noted:

> He was a hearty, full-blooded fellow, the very opposite to me in most
> respects; but we found we had some subjects in common, and it was a
> bond of union when I learned that he was as friendless as I.[9]

We have considered him earlier (p. 22) as a possible first lover of Holmes, as perhaps being the man in the affair that sent Holmes off on that first, hastier visit to France, to end an undesired and embarrassing pregnancy in the complete privacy of another country. If that first lover were Trevor, then it is unlikely that Holmes would have succumbed a second time to his attractions— unlikely, but not impossible. Yet a meeting after a long gap of years—since, indeed, the very beginning of Holmes's career—would have been a much more probable prelude to a romantic episode.

A chance reunion with Reginald Musgrave, whether or not that gentle aristocrat remained unmarried (and, with his sense of family responsibility, it is unlikely that he would have still remained a bachelor), would have been a much less likely start to an affair. Although handsome, Musgrave was not the sort to retain any strong sexual attraction after a dozen years. He, we feel, can be eliminated; but Victor Trevor remains a strong possibility.

Musgrave and Victor Trevor are but two candidates. Other males, mentioned in passing or not mentioned at all in the chronicles, may be imagined as lovers. However, we believe we have found evidence that points clearly towards someone—and he a major figure in Holmes's career.

Let us examine that final encounter between Holmes and Colonel Sebastian Moran, following the latter's capture by Inspector Lestrade:

"You fiend!" [Moran] kept on muttering. "You clever, clever fiend!"[10]

Then comes one of those peculiar exchanges that become explicable only when our thesis is borne in mind:

"Ah, colonel," said Holmes, arranging his rumpled collar, "journeys end in lovers' meetings, as the old play says. I don't think I have had the pleasure of seeing you since you favoured me with those attentions as I lay on the ledge above the Reichenbach Falls."[11]

To which the Colonel, still staring at Holmes "like a man in a trance," can only respond:

"You cunning, cunning fiend!"[12]

We may notice that, even while wreaking vengeance upon his former lover (if our deduction be correct), Holmes is still unable to resist that feminine instinct to tidy him up by rearranging his collar!

"Journeys end in lovers' meetings." Sherlock's reunion with Colonel Sebastian Moran. (The Empty House)

Well, to say the least, the Colonel appears a likely candidate; but the evidence is not, as we recognize, conclusive. This question will be re-examined in a later chapter.

When that first affair had brought its predictable but, for Holmes, unfortunate consequence, the visit to France had been rapidly arranged and Holmes's recovery had been swift, even if it had left him deeply depressed. On this second occasion the journey was carefully planned, not only for the opportunity it provided for avoiding the vengeance of Professor Moriarty but also to enable Holmes to drop out of sight for an unspecified period—several years, at least.

Why did he decide to vanish for so long? On that first occasion when Holmes went to France, the pregnancy had been ended (by whatever means) in a brief enough time. The difference is so marked that it indicates a difference in intent. It seems likely that Holmes's aim, on the first occasion, had been to get rid of the baby; on the second, however, we believe he wished to experience the pleasures of maternity, at least for a while—even if that could only be done covertly, for he would not wish to "burn his boats" or even to tarnish his burgeoning reputation. Holmes must have shuddered at the very idea of the amusement of Inspector Lestrade and others, had the "great detective" been exposed as a mere woman!

What went wrong? Why did Holmes return eventually to London? Was it because he was finding the task of rearing a child to be quite a bore and missing the continual stimulus of his exacting profession? Was it because he was pining for Watson? Was it because this second accouchement had produced only a still-born child, yet had been so physically disastrous as to delay greatly a return that might otherwise have taken place earlier? Or was it because Holmes's child died young, as was so sadly common in Victorian times?

It should be noted that earlier commentators have found reason to believe that Holmes *did* have a child, even if they have mistaken Holmes's particular role in that child's production. Indeed, an identity for Holmes's child has been suggested, in the ample person of that very talented American detective Nero Wolfe. It is true that Wolfe's combination of massive rotundity, physical indolence and extreme mental alertness do very much suggest, not Sherlock, but Mycroft; a likely enough consequence of heredity.[13] For our part, however, we regard the evidence for a Yugoslavian (Montenegrin) origin of Nero to be overwhelming. Moreover, a visit to Yugoslavia during those alleged travels was not among Holmes's claims!

Well, then, was the pregnancy ended artificially or did it end naturally, in the birth of a still-born or living child; and, if the child were living, for how long? These are questions we do not pretend to be able to answer conclusively. Unless new evidence is forthcoming, no definite conclusions can be drawn. Whatever exactly happened, it is generally recognized by commentators on the Canon that Holmes was never the same after his return.[14] This could, of course, equally well be the consequence of having a pregnancy terminated prematurely or of having—and losing—a child.

In general, as we must confess, Sherlock Holmes's ruses have succeeded. Though we are confident we are closer to the truth than was Watson, we also are left with certain problems we cannot solve.

The Years Together

The Empty House

BEFORE THIS ADVENTURE TOOK PLACE, Watson had not only suffered the supposed loss of his friend but also a genuine bereavement. Though it is usually presumed that this was the death of his wife, the name of the deceased person was never made explicit. It could have been Watson's mother, his father or his brother, for all that the chronicle tells us.

If it was indeed Watson's wife, it is perhaps surprising that Holmes did not return sooner. Certainly it is remarkable that Holmes took so long even to mention the happening. Not until he had given that lengthy account of his escape from the Reichenbach Falls and of his alleged doings during his three year absence did Holmes raise the matter, and then only obliquely:

> In some manner he had learned of my own sad bereavement, and
> his sympathy was shown in his manner rather than his words. "Work is
> the best antidote to sorrow, my dear Watson," said he....[1]

In view of Holmes's evident antipathy towards Mrs. Mary Watson, this may constitute the most direct evidence we have as to the identity of the deceased!

Thus, with the arrest of Colonel Sebastian Moran, did Holmes re-establish himself in his old quarters in Baker Street, laying the foundations for a third—and for a while, as we believe, more mutually fulfilling—relationship with Watson.

Wisteria Lodge

By the beginning of this adventure, by our chronology within two months of the Return, we consider that Watson had also returned to his old Baker Street quarters. This is not made explicit, but Watson's statement, at its commencement, that "we sat at our lunch"[2] is not one that would come naturally to a guest, while Holmes's:

> "But here, unless I am mistaken, is our client." [3]

"our client,"—be it noted—suggests at very least a resumed mutuality of concern.

The Holmes of the Return, whatever his physical condition, shows signs of being much mellower—even, at times, more mischievous—than the old. First of all, we may recall the "old book collector" joke that he had played upon Watson—even if, afterwards, to feel some remorse at its effects—at the moment of that return.[4] Here we have another example of good-humoured teasing:

> [Holmes] read the telegram aloud.
> "Have just had the most incredible and grotesque experience. May I consult you?—Scott Eccles, Post Office, Charing Cross."
> "Man or woman?" I asked.
> "Oh, man, of course. No woman would ever send a reply-paid telegram. She would have come."[5]

Furthermore, we find ourselves having to shed our image of Holmes the urbanite, the man who was happy only in the city, and substitute instead the unfamiliar one of Holmes the nature-lover. When they visit Esher:

> "I'm sure, Watson, a week in the country will be invaluable to you," he remarked. "It is very pleasant to see the first green shoots upon the hedges and the catkins on the hazels once again. With a spud, a tin box, and an elementary book on botany, there are instructive days to be spent." He prowled about with this equipment himself, but it was a poor show of plants which he would bring back of an evening.[6]

There is a decidedly feminine, almost a maternal note in Holmes's first sentence. However, it is apparent that Watson did not much share Holmes's new botanical enthusiasms!

Mr. Scott Eccles strikes something of a new note, though not at first. He is described initially thus:

> ...a stout, tall, grey-whiskered and solemnly respectable person was ushered into the room. His life history was written in his heavy features and pompous manner. From his spats to his gold-rimmed spectacles he was a Conservative, a Churchman, a good citizen, orthodox and conventional to the last degree.[7]

But was he? We find reason to doubt it!

> "I am a bachelor," said he, "and, being of a sociable turn, I cultivate a large number of friends. Among these are the family of a retired brewer called Melville, living at...Kensington. It was at his table that I met some weeks ago a young fellow named Garcia. He was, I understand, of Spanish descent and connected in some way with the Embassy. He spoke perfect English, was pleasing in his manners, and as good-looking a man as ever I saw in my life.
>
> , "In some way we struck up quite a friendship, this young fellow and I. He seemed to take a fancy to me from the first, and within two days of our meeting he came to see me at Lee. One thing led to another, and it ended with his inviting me to spend a few days at his house...."[8]

A more classic description of a homosexual encounter, and its rapid development into an affair, could scarcely be found! There is this "orthodox and conventional" person, stressing so heavily the physical attractions of his new-found, much younger friend; there is that second meeting, arranged within two days; and there is that rapid follow-up visit, planned for a longer period—even though this did not, in fact, transpire. Is more evidence necessary? Very well, then.

"Our dinner was tete-a-tete," Eccles notes, and goes on to recount that:

> "About eleven I was glad to go to bed. Some time later Garcia looked in at my door—the room was dark at the time—and asked me if I had rung. I said that I had not. He apologized for having disturbed me so late, saying it was nearly one o'clock."[9]

and subsequently he notes that his host "had shown me which was his bedroom the night before."[10]

It is evident that Garcia, having given a hint that was not followed up, waited awhile before seeking his guest, only to suffer a more direct rebuff. Was that a factor in his vanishing before the next morning?

We may recall also how Garcia had remarked "what a queer household [his] was to find in the heart of Surrey" and how Scott Eccles had commented that "it proved a great deal queerer than I thought."[11] Well, maybe that particular adjective did not have the connotations in 1894 that it was to gain later. Yet it is surprising that Watson, even with his medical experience, does not seem to have perceived anything strange in Eccles's account.

Holmes, however, was as usual more percipient:

> "There is," he said, "on the face of it something unnatural about this strange and sudden friendship between the young Spaniard and Scott Eccles. It was the former who forced the pace."[12]

Perceiving the situation as he so clearly did, what was Holmes's reaction to it? Having made his comment, Holmes goes out of his way to avoid shocking Watson, inventing quite other reasons for the friendship. These satisfied Watson, however little they may convince us. Otherwise, Holmes's attitude seems complaisant. He is unfailingly polite to Mr. Eccles—but, we may note, he does not invite Eccles back for any explanation of what happened. Instead, the client is allowed simply to vanish unsatisfied—perhaps doubly so!—from the case.

The Norwood Builder

Watson notes at the outset of this adventure:

> At the time of which I speak, Holmes had been back for some months, and I, at his request, had sold my practice and returned to share the old quarters in Baker Street.[13]

Thus we can begin to appreciate the value Holmes placed upon Watson's continued presence in his life. This is stressed by what follows:

> A young doctor, named Verner, had purchased my Kensington practice, and given with astonishingly little demur the highest price

that I ventured to ask—an incident which only explained itself some years later, when I found that Verner was a distant relation of Holmes, and that it was my friend who had really found the money.[14]

How did Watson discover this? Obviously he was not told by Holmes. Was Watson developing his own deductive powers, as consequence of their increasingly intimate association? Did Watson perceive belatedly that there was some physical similarity between Verner and Holmes? Did Watson happen upon some letter, or receipt, that revealed the truth? Or was it simply that the close relationship which had developed between Holmes and Watson meant that Watson could know, with absolute certainty, how Holmes would have arranged the affair?

Again we may note Holmes's new benignity. After having grumbled at the lack of interesting cases coming to hand since "the death of the late lamented Professor Moriarty," he pushes back his chair and says with a smile:

"Well, well, I must not be selfish."[15]

No; even if his abilities are yet undimmed, this is not the old nervous Holmes, using drugs to relieve his tensions. Instead it is a much more tranquil and good-humoured, even whimsical, person.

The Golden Pince-Nez

At the commencement of this adventure, Watson gives a list of never-to-be-chronicled cases that show the depth of his involvement in Holmes's adventures. The domestic scene that Watson sketches portrays a relaxed relationship:

It was a wild, tempestuous night towards the close of November. Holmes and I sat together in silence all the evening, he engaged with a powerful lens deciphering the remains of the original inscription upon a palimpsest, I deep in a recent treatise upon surgery.[16]

The palimpsest in question—revealed by Holmes's study to be "an Abbey's accounts dating from the second half of the fifteenth century"[17]—was obviously being examined by Holmes either as a mental exercise or in the hope of some discovery of greater historical importance. In either instance, Holmes's study of it shows him to have been taking up what can only be called 'hobbies'—

quite a change from his earlier exclusive concern with criminous matters. Equally
clearly, though Watson had sold his practice, he had not yet entirely given up his
medical ambitions.

It is interesting to find Watson noting:

> I may have remarked before that Holmes had, when he liked, a peculiarly
> ingratiating way with women, and that he very readily established terms
> of confidence with them. [Soon] he had captured the housekeeper's
> goodwill, and was chatting with her as if he had known her for years.[18]

Such a ready establishment of relationship would, of course, be much easier for
another woman. The fact that Watson does not perceive this indicates that he
was himself still unaware of Holmes's femininity.

The Three Students

At the beginning of this adventure Holmes and Watson had travelled, for
unexplained reasons, to "one of our great University towns" and had stayed
on there while Holmes pursued "some laborious researches in Early English
charters."[19] Yet, as Watson notes:

> My friend's temper had not improved since he had been deprived of
> the congenial surroundings of Baker Street.[20]

This is an unexpected reaction in one so professedly able to withstand the
extreme hardships of travel in such places as Tibet and nineteenth-century
Arabia. It casts further doubt upon the reality of those vaunted adventures of
the Hiatus! Rather, we may suggest that Holmes found his lifelong pose easier
to sustain in a familiar environment, an environment that provided him with a
secure retreat.

The Solitary Cyclist

When a personable client arrived late one Saturday evening at 221B Baker Street:

> My friend took the lady's ungloved hand and examined it with
> as close an attention and as little sentiment as a scientist would show
> to a specimen.[21]

Sherlock's encounter with Mr. Woodley, as described to Watson and here depicted, scarcely accords with the facts! (The Solitary Cyclist)

In contrast, Watson is much attracted by "the young, beautiful woman" Violet Hunter, "tall, graceful and queenly" as she is. He is surprised that Holmes does not react similarly and, once again, is obviously still unaware of Holmes's sex. Once again we, knowing the truth, need not share Watson's surprise.

In this adventure, Holmes arrives back at 221B "with a cut lip and a discoloured lump upon his forehead."[22] In his account of what happened, he says:

> "You are aware that I have some proficiency in the good old British sport of boxing.... It was a straight left against a slogging ruffian. I emerged as you see me. Mr. Woodley went home in a cart."[23]

This is another occasion when Holmes is involved in offstage physical violence and when the only account of the events is his own. It is noteworthy that, when Watson and Holmes encounter Woodley together later in the adventure, there is no least indication to suggest that Woodley had suffered more than Holmes had.[24] Instead, Woodley is initially quite undismayed by that second encounter with Holmes, showing none of the apprehension that might have resulted from so sound a thrashing as that which Holmes claimed to have administered. Could it be that it was Holmes who had suffered most in that combat?

Black Peter

This adventure forms an interesting counterpoint to the last. Here, Holmes is involved in a violent encounter on-stage, but shows little pugilistic skill. Even after Holmes has deftly handcuffed Patrick Cairns, that latter gentleman, to quote Watson:

> ...would have quickly overpowered my friend had Hopkins and I not rushed to his rescue.[25]

There are, of course, his exercises with the harpoon[26] to show that Holmes was quite strong—a matter we have never doubted. Yet, when the violence is on-stage and Holmes is involved directly, he seems always to need rescuing!

The Bruce-Partington Plans

At the time of this adventure, the relationship between Holmes and Watson is clearly changing again. First, let us note an exchange respecting brother

Mycroft, upon whose power in the British political scene Holmes lays stress. When Watson observes:

> "You told me that he had some small office under the British Government."

Holmes responds by chuckling:

> "I did not know you quite so well in those days."[27]

When Holmes and Watson go forth together to keep watch in Caulfield Gardens, even Watson becomes aware of the change:

> ...for a moment I saw something in his eyes which was nearer to tenderness than I had ever seen.[28]

"Tenderness"—a curious word to use concerning the affection of one man for another, but very natural between one sex and another. We believe that this was the time when Watson came to learn, at last, the true nature of Holmes, the feminine nature that had been so successfully concealed from him for so long.

Holmes's liking for jewellery is again evident here. He spends a day at Windsor and returns with "a remarkably fine emerald tie-pin."[29] It seems a little unfair to Watson that, after his reasonably prominent and courageous part in this adventure, he was not even invited along to meet that "certain gracious lady." But then Holmes rarely shared credit with his partner.

The Veiled Lodger

From the time Holmes meets Eugenia Ronder, he shows her a great deal of courtesy until, at the end of the case, she lifts her veil to display her savaged face. His reaction?

> Holmes held up his hand in a gesture of pity and protest, and together we left the room.[30]

Not a comment, then, from Holmes; and not even a farewell word. Evidently there were some things that exceeded Holmes's (and Watson's) sensibilities. We might compare this scene with that in which Queen Alexandra was shown the face of Joseph Merrick, the so-called 'Elephant Man.' Having been warned that his appearance was literally "shocking" she was nevertheless able to enter his room "with a relaxed grace, [she] smiled and took the introduction with perfect serenity."[31]

We feel Holmes scarcely merited the credit he took for convincing Mrs. Ronder that suicide was not a morally permissible option. We wonder what Holmes would have done in like circumstance.

The Sussex Vampire

Here again, Holmes displays a form of behaviour at the end of this case that might be viewed as unduly harsh. Of the fifteen-year-old lad who had been poisoning his baby step-brother, Holmes says:

> "I think a year at sea would be my prescription for Master Jacky."[32]

A common enough prescription in the late Victorian years, to be sure: parents were able to learn details in the book 'How To Send A Boy To Sea,' published by Warne at one shilling and often recommended in the Correspondence columns of *The Boy's Own Paper*. For a child as high-strung and sensitive as young Ferguson, however, a year's exposure to a life at sea could have amounted to a death sentence. Indeed, it might perhaps have subjected him to a fate worse than death.

The Missing Three-Quarter

Here, Holmes's ignorance of sport is much in evidence. He is wholly uncomprehending of, if amused by, Cyril Overton's outpourings[33] and turns in vain to his files to try to gain understanding of them. Had Holmes attended an English public school, such a lack of knowledge would have been inconceivable. Indeed, could any man who had grown up in England—even if privately tutored, and however little interested in sport he might be—remain so ignorant?

Watson had sold his medical practice only two years before and, as we have seen (p. 64), continued to read medical textbooks after that severance. It is thus somewhat surprising to find him commenting:

> It argues the degree in which I had lost touch with my profession that the name of Leslie Armstrong was unknown to me.[34]

Some time during those two years, then, Watson had abandoned his medical ambitions and committed himself wholly to his partnership with Holmes.

Notice also Holmes's wifely-sounding admonitions:

> "Early to bed to-night, Watson, for I foresee that tomorrow may be an eventful day."[35]

and:

> "Eat a good breakfast, Watson, for I propose to set upon Dr. Armstrong's trail to-day...."[36]

There is also that curious comment to Watson, as Holmes examines a blotting-pad:

> "It is a pity he did not write in pencil.... As you have no doubt frequently observed, Watson, the impression usually goes through—a fact which has dissolved many a happy marriage."[37]

It is a comment that provides a fruitful basis for conjecture!

The Aging Holmes

THE CHANGING RELATIONSHIP between Holmes and Watson is well illustrated here. At the outset of this adventure, Watson is asleep when Holmes awakens him, being already at the bedside with a lighted candle.[1] Prior to this time, Holmes would never have entered Watson's room without knocking. The fact that he does so, and without apology, says much about the changed situation.

Or was it only Watson's room by then? At a later stage in the adventure, Watson mentions their return to "our room."[2] Was he meaning their sitting-room? Or was it that they were sharing a bedroom?

After many cases during which we have seen Holmes in a mood of general benignity, it is a shock—and an indication of another alteration in their relationship—to encounter Holmes in a thoroughly bad temper early in the morning, before any particular problems can have ruffled him:

> "...and I must admit, Watson, that you have some power of selection which atones for much which I deplore in your narratives. Your fatal habit of looking at everything from the point of view of a story instead of as a scientific exercise has ruined what might have been an instructive and even classical series of demonstrations. You slur over work of the

"Come, Watson, come.... The game is afoot." Sherlock enters Watson's bedroom—and without knocking! (Abbey Grange)

utmost finesse and delicacy, in order to dwell upon sensational details which may excite but cannot possibly instruct the reader."

To which Watson responds, in justifiable indignation:

"Why do you not write them yourself?"[3]

But Holmes, instead of apologizing, adds insult to injury by being condescending:

"I will, my dear Watson, I will."[4]

This irritability serves as warning of Holmes's deteriorating physical condition, well demonstrated in the next case.

The Devil's Foot

This adventure finds Holmes and Watson together in a small cottage in Cornwall. Holmes's "iron constitution" has, it seems, come near to giving way "in the face of hard work of a most exacting kind, aggravated, perhaps, by occasional indiscretions of his own."[5]

Since Watson had weaned Holmes away from drugs by this time, just what were those indiscretions? Although Watson begins the tale with a reference to his "long and intimate friendship"[6] with Holmes, we do not necessarily have to associate Watson with them! However, that by then there *was* intimacy—in the fullest modern sense of the word—we do not doubt.

Was Watson being literally correct in diagnosing a deficiency of iron as the cause of Holmes's medical problems? This was a day when millions of Victorian women purchased quantities of iron-enriched alcohol blood tonics to relieve the symptoms, at least, of that most chronic of Victorian complaints: Female Trouble. Could Holmes have been, at age forty-three (if the normal calculation of his birth year, 1854, is accepted), already approaching menopause?

Two other points are worthy of notice. First of all, when the two of them inhale the terrible fumes of the Devil's Foot, it is Watson who rescues Holmes from death, not the converse;[7] yet another indication that the detective was not so physically tough as he claimed.

Secondly, at the end of the adventure, Holmes states:

"I have never loved, Watson...."[8]

Well, perhaps not with the warmth of some fortunate marriages, but....

The Disappearance of Lady Frances Carfax

This case sees Watson sent abroad to act as dogsbody for Holmes. Though Watson tries hard to please, his reward is to be harangued on his shortcomings—predictably, in view of Holmes's continuing phase of physical problems and consequent irritability. Indeed, Watson's absence—though initially desired—may eventually have added to that irritability:

"A very pretty hash you have made of it! I rather think you had better come back with me to London by the night express.... I cannot recall any possible blunder which you have omitted. The total effect of your proceedings has been to give the alarm everywhere and yet to discover nothing."[9]

Once again, Watson is understandably bitter:

> "Perhaps you would have done no better."

And, once again, Holmes's smug reply is calculated to enhance, rather than to remedy, Watson's bitterness:

> "There is no 'perhaps' about it. I *have* done better...."[10]

At the outset of the adventure, Holmes shows some curiosity about Watson's companion on the cab-ride, but never quite asks who it was.[11] Watson is relieved when the topic is apparently abandoned—so relieved, indeed, that we must presume the companion was feminine.[12] Was it to remove Watson from that companionship that Holmes sent him off abroad?

All in all, in this case, Holmes is seen at his least endearing. It is satisfying, therefore, to find him admitting at the end, if rather grudgingly, that he also has not done well. Indeed, he says:

> "Should you care to add the case to your annals, my dear Watson, it can only be as an example of that temporary eclipse to which even the best-balanced mind may be exposed."[13]

The Dancing Men

> "Your chequebook," says Holmes to Watson, "is locked in my drawer, and you have not asked for the key."[14]

Perhaps no better example exists of Holmes's proprietary attitude to Watson. These are the words of a wife who, once too often, has lost her household expenses to the turf or to her husband's gaming wagers. We know that Watson had been a gambling man, but we do not know how long he maintained that habit. Was there a resurgence, against which Holmes was taking precautions? It seems likely enough, from what transpires in a later adventure (see p. 87).

However, even a wife would be unlikely to object to an occasional game of billiards. Though Watson's opponent, Thurston, was probably the noted billiard player and billiard-table manufacturer John Thurston, such a game would have cost little enough. As Michael Harrison has noted:

"Cut out the poetry, Watson." Holmes is relaxing, but in bitter mood. (The Retired Colourman)

The standard charge for billiards in the 1880's was 1s. an hour by the day, or 1s 6d an hour by gaslight.[15]

The Retired Colourman

"Melancholy and philosophic"[16] was the way Watson described Holmes's mood in this case. He jokes bitterly about his profession (for the first time, we might note), pretending to equate his practice with that of a quack doctor.[17] He lounges lengthily in his armchair, quite drained of his normal energy.[18]

Watson attempts to lighten the atmosphere with an overly flowery description of The Haven, Josiah Amberley's house:

> "I think it would interest you, Holmes. It is like some penurious patrician who has sunk into the company of his inferiors. You know that particular quarter, the monotonous brick streets, the weary suburban highways. Right in the middle of them, a little island of culture and comfort, lies this old home, surrounded by a high sun-baked wall mottled with lichens and topped with moss, the sort of wall...."

This is met only with the sour interruption:

"Cut out the poetry, Watson."[19]

Charles Augustus Milverton

Two of Watson's responses to Holmes seem to us to confirm that, by this time, Watson was well aware of Holmes's masquerade. First of all, when Holmes says:

"You would not call me a marrying man, Watson?"

The reply is unhesitating and emphatic:

"No, indeed!"[20]

Then there is the rather odd answer by Watson to Holmes's later question:

"...Since it is morally justifiable [to burgle Milverton's house], I have only to consider the question of personal risk. Surely a gentleman should not lay much stress upon this when a lady is in most desperate need of his help?"

Watson responds:

"You will be in such a false position."[21]

We expect that Watson laid heavy stress upon that first word!

It is possible that there is more to be read into these exchanges. Had menopause caused Holmes to end their brief physical relationship and, in consequence, to strive again to bolster his own chosen masculine role? Was there a consequent irony in Watson's response? Because of what follows, we do not think so; but we are on unsafe ground here and prefer not to tread it further.

Certainly we may note a changed attitude of Watson to Holmes. When Holmes makes it clear that he is going ahead with the burglary, Watson is firm with him:

"Well, I don't like it, but I suppose it must be. When do we start?"
"You are not coming."

"Then you are not going. I give you my word of honour—and I never broke it in my life—that I will take a cab straight to the police-station and give you away unless you let me share this adventure with you."

"You can't help me."

"How do you know that? You can't tell what may happen. Anyway, my resolution is taken. Other people beside you have self-respect and even reputations."

Holmes had looked annoyed, but his brow cleared, and he clapped me on the shoulder.

"Well, well, my dear fellow, be it so. We have shared the same room for some years, and it would be amusing if we ended by sharing the same cell."[22]

Never hitherto has Watson been so downright in his dealings with Holmes; never has Holmes's capitulation been so swift and so complete. Has the sharing of rooms caused this transformation?

Early in this case, Holmes threatens physical violence on Milverton, but is quickly cowed when Milverton places his hand on the hilt of his revolver, without even drawing it.[23] We hasten to note that we do not cite this as an example of feminine pusillanimity, but to demonstrate once again that Holmes was not the capable scrapper that he claimed to be.

Most surprising of all in this case, perhaps, is Holmes's sudden seeking of the reassurance of physical contact, while Watson and he are hiding behind the curtain in Milverton's study:

I felt Holmes's hand steal into mine and give me a reassuring shake...."[24]

The Hound of the Baskervilles

As one reads this case, one perceives again that Watson is assuming a somewhat more equal role in the relationship and that Holmes is not unhappy with the changed situation. Indeed, Holmes's complacency about it is made evident by a remark so quickly passed over that it has escaped attention hitherto:

"Excellent! This is a colleague, Watson, after our own heart."[25]

A reversed illustration. Above, *the illustration as published. Watson's jacket is buttoned the wrong way and the traffic is (in English terms!) on the wrong side of the street.* Opposite, *the corrected illustration. Note that Watson is now politely in the man's position, on the outside of the pavement [i.e. sidewalk]. Illustrator Sidney Paget's initials are missing—probably blocked out to help conceal the error.* (The Hound of the Baskervilles)

Not "our hearts," be it noted, but "our heart." No more telling phrase exists in the entire Canon!

Consider also the degree of anxiety expressed by Holmes about Watson during this adventure. Before Watson even leaves Baker Street for his journey, Holmes is worrying:

> "I can only wish you better luck in Devonshire. But I'm not easy in my mind about it."
>
> "About what?"
>
> "About sending you. It's an ugly business, Watson, an ugly, dangerous business, and the more I see of it the less I like it. Yes, my dear fellow, you may laugh, but I give you my word that I shall be very glad to have you back safe and sound in Baker Street once more."[26]

Notice the quick, feminine resentment at Watson's dismissal of the danger and the possessiveness evident in the last sentence.

When they meet again on the moor, though Holmes has been living rough for a number of days, he has not sprouted any beard. No indeed; "his chin" is "as smooth...as if he were in Baker Street."[27] Hardly surprising when he had no need to shave—and one of the strongest pieces of evidence for the interpretation we are advocating!

See also how Holmes, when he perceives how his deceptions have angered Watson, sets out with a typically feminine skill to soothe and to flatter him:

> "Then you use me, and yet do not trust me!" I cried, with some bitterness. "I think that I have deserved better at your hands, Holmes."
>
> "My dear fellow, you have been invaluable to me in this as in many other cases, and I beg that you will forgive me if I have seemed to play a trick upon you. In truth, it was partly for your own sake that I did it, and it was my appreciation of the danger which you ran which led me to come down and examine the matter for myself...."[28]

But Watson is still far from happy, so Holmes continues the treatment with greater success:

> "Then my reports have all been wasted!" My voice trembled as I recalled the pains and the pride with which I had composed them.
>
> Holmes took a bundle of papers from his pocket.

Sherlock roughing it, and razorless, Dartmoor—yet his chin, as Watson noted, was "as smooth...as if he were in Baker Street." (The Hound of the Baskervilles)

"Here are your reports, my deal fellow, and very well thumbed, I assure you. I made excellent arrangements, and they are only delayed one day upon their way. I must compliment you exceedingly upon the zeal and the intelligence which you have shown over an extraordinarily difficult case."

I was still rather raw over the deception which had been practised upon me, but the warmth of Holmes's praise drove my anger from my mind. I felt also in my heart that he was right in what he said, and that

Sherlock about to offer sympathy to another woman. (The Hound of the Baskervilles)

it was really best for our purpose that I should not have known that he was upon the moor.

"That's better," said he, seeing the shadow rise from my face.[29]

And after that extremely feminine comment, Holmes proceeds briskly to other business before Watson becomes aware of how he has been manipulated.

In this case also, we see Holmes's swift and strong sympathy with another woman in trouble. When he sees the mark of the whip on the neck of Mrs. Stapleton, and before he has become aware of the other injuries she has suffered, he cries out:

"The brute!"

before quickly taking charge of ministering to her.[30] Moreover, although Mrs. Stapleton's part in the plot is equivocal, to say the least, she retains Holmes's sympathy and is given immediate opportunity to atone.

The Six Napoleons

Watson has a separate bedroom at the time of this adventure. However, Holmes enters it unhesitatingly, after the briefest of taps at the door and without awaiting an invitation. Moreover, even though Watson is "still dressing," Holmes does not retire but feels sufficiently at ease to proceed to read to him a telegram.[31]

Later in this case, we do see Holmes in physical action—though, be it said, with Watson and Lestrade in close support! And how does he attack? Not face to face, in classic manly British fashion, but by leaping on the criminal's back with what Watson describes as "the bound of a tiger"[32]—a feline image for a feminine mode of attack!

We may remark Holmes's reaction to the congratulations he receives at the dramatic denouement of this adventure:

> "Gentlemen," he cried, "let me introduce you to the famous black pearl of the Borgias!"

At the applause of Watson and Lestrade:

> A flush of colour sprang to Holmes's pale cheeks, and he bowed to us like the master dramatist who receives the homage of his audience.

When Lestrade congratulates him further:

> "Thank you!" said Holmes. "Thank you!" and as he turned away it seemed to me that he was more nearly moved by the softer human emotions than I had ever seen him.[33]

Well, Watson may have been not remembering Holmes's earlier expressions of emotion very clearly; but Holmes *was* indeed changing!

The Problem of Thor Bridge

At the outset of this adventure, we learn that Holmes has been starved of investigations for a while. Watson comes downstairs expecting to find him "in depressed spirits." Instead, Holmes proves to be "in a mood particularly bright and joyous," indeed exhibiting "that somewhat sinister cheerfulness which was characteristic of his brighter moments."[34] Consequently, Watson deduces correctly that Holmes has a case and is congratulated in typically Holmesian fashion:

> "The faculty of deduction is certainly contagious, Watson. It has enabled you to probe my secret. Yes, I have a case."[35]

Now, if we were to consider that second sentence in isolation…. But we will resist that temptation and merely remark that the Baker Street establishment is doing well, for it now boasts both a cook[36] and a page, Billy;[37] so the lack of investigations cannot have seriously affected Holmes's finances. Moreover, when the Gold King, Neil Gibson, invites him to "Name your figure," Holmes responds coldly:

> "My professional charges are upon a fixed scale…I do not vary them, save when I remit them altogether."[38]

This adventure reveals little concerning Holmes's relationship with Watson, but it does indicate Holmes's rather odd response to a triangular love affair. When Neil Gibson admits his love for Grace Dunbar, Holmes treats him harshly:

> "…I never wanted anything more than the love and possession of that woman. I told her so."
>
> "Oh, you did, did you?"
>
> Holmes could look very formidable when he was moved.
>
> "I said to her that if I could marry her I would, but that it was out of my power. I said that money was no object and that all I could do to make her happy and comfortable would be done."
>
> "Very generous, I am sure," said Holmes, with a sneer.
>
> "See here, Mr. Holmes. I came to you on a question of evidence, not on a question of morals. I'm not asking for your criticism."
>
> "It is only for the young lady's sake that I touch your case at all," said Holmes sternly. "I don't know that anything she is accused of is really

Sherlock was without mercy in dealing with men who had 'trifled with' other women.
(Thor Bridge)

worse than what you have yourself admitted, that you have tried to ruin a defenseless girl who was under your roof. Some of you rich men have to be taught that all the world cannot be bribed into condoning your offenses."[39]

Whilst Victorian Puritanism was indeed extreme, it is surprising that Holmes shared it to such a degree that he considered a not-very-determined attempt at seduction to be as serious as murder!

In contrast, let us consider Holmes's reaction when he encounters Miss Dunbar in the prison cell. His favourable response to her is immediate:

> "...you need not pain yourself by entering into that part of the story [her relationship with Gibson]. After seeing you I am prepared to accept Mr. Gibson's statement both as to the influence which you had over him and as to the innocence of your relations with him."[40]

Was it that in Miss Dunbar, "tall" and with a "commanding presence," Holmes found an echo of himself?

Moreover, is it not curious that Holmes should describe Gibson's wife's feelings for her husband as a "perverted love"?[41] Indeed, Holmes seems unnecessarily perturbed by the thought of Mrs. Gibson's "too demonstrative affection" and to forgive quite readily her husband's attempts to repel it.[42] Surely this is a curious attitude to married love! However, it becomes comprehensible in view of Holmes's own cold temperament.

The Priory School

With this case we enter a new century and a seeming new awareness on Watson's part that he and Holmes are growing older. At the beginning, he notes:

> We have had some dramatic entrances and exits upon our small stage at Baker Street....[43]

a quotation from Jacques' famous meditation on the "seven ages of Man" in Shakespeare's *As You Like It*.[44] Holmes himself remarks that change also, and pays Watson the honour of admitting him to an equal partnership, when he says:

"...perhaps the scent is not so cold but that two old hounds like Watson and myself may get a sniff of it."[45]

Shoscombe Old Place

Here Watson admits that he is again—or is it still?—betting regularly. Holmes asks:

"By the way, Watson, you know something of racing?"

a somewhat surprising question, one feels, after so long an acquaintance; but perhaps he was being facetious! In any case, Watson responds:

"I ought to. I pay for it with about half my wound pension."[46]

Yet Holmes had not only exhibited a considerable knowledge of horse-racing in an earlier adventure,[47] but also shows a continuing knowledge in this one, when he refers so glibly to the "Handy Guide to the Turf."[48]

Later on, Watson is quite respectfully asked his opinion on a bone. He replies:

"It's the upper condyle of a human femur."
"Exactly!" responds Holmes.[49]

Yet, as Dr. Samuel R. Meaker has pointed out,[50] the human femur does not have an upper condyle. So it seems not only that Watson's medical knowledge was becoming rusty, but also that Holmes's anatomical knowledge was by then equally weak! Well, their years of tuition—or, in Holmes's case, of self-tuition—were far behind....

The Three Garridebs

This adventure contains two particularly informative passages. At the very beginning, Watson writes:

I remember the date very well, for it was in the same month that Holmes refused a knighthood for services which may some day be described. I only refer to the matter in passing, for in my position of partner and confidant I am obliged to be particularly careful to avoid any indiscretion. I repeat, however, that this enables me to fix the date, which was the latter end of June, 1902, shortly after the conclusion of the South African War. Holmes had spent several days in bed, as was his habit from time to time....[51]

This passage repays careful analysis. Most other chroniclers would have written "It was in the same year..."; yet Watson thinks in terms of months—and, of course, in the life of any mixed couple, there is a regular monthly cycle to be taken into account! Moreover, we may note that Holmes had just emerged from "several days in bed." Well, he was forty-eight years old by then and the female cycle can, in its waning stages, attain a particular severity. Or was it simply that, in the earlier stages of his partnership with Watson, Holmes was less willing, because of the role he was adopting and Watson's ignorance of it, to allow himself to succumb to equally severe physical discomforts by seeking his bed?

At such an age, it might have been very appropriate for a Victorian gentleman to accept the accolade of a knighthood; but Holmes could not, for the reason that we know. It was one thing to have received an emerald tie-pin from the recently deceased Queen Empress[52] or to have accepted the *Légion d'Honneur* for his achievements in France;[53] but to accept a *knighthood*—why, that would have been fraud; and Holmes was a bastion of the Law, not a lawbreaker!

The second, particularly illuminating passage comes near the end of the adventure, when we witness Holmes's emotions after Watson has been shot:

> "You're not hurt, Watson? For God's sake, say that you are not hurt!"
>
> It was worth a wound—it was worth many wounds—to know the depth of loyalty and love which lay behind that cold mask. The clear, hard eyes were dimmed for a moment, and the firm lips were shaking. For the one and only time I caught a glimpse of a great heart as well as of a great brain. All my years of humble but single-minded service culminated in that moment of revelation.
>
> "It's nothing, Holmes. It's a mere scratch."
>
> He had ripped up my trousers with his pocket-knife.
>
> "You are right," he cried, with an immense sigh of relief. "It is quite superficial." His face set like flint as he glared at our prisoner, who was

sitting up with a dazed face. "By the Lord, it is as well for you. If you had killed Watson, you would not have got out of this room alive."[54]

One is left wondering just where that wound was, when Holmes had to rip up Watson's trousers with a pocket-knife to examine it? Was its location likely to have been such as to cause Holmes a special and particular concern?

Yet this scene remains a vivid reminder of the relationship between Holmes and Watson, one which might profitably be studied to help in understanding the contrast between "that cold mask" and Watson's endearing, naive devotion. Certainly Watson gave much, but received little in return.

The Parting of the Ways

The Illustrious Client

SOME TIME BETWEEN JULY AND SEPTEMBER of 1902, there must have been a serious quarrel between Holmes and Watson—serious enough to cause Watson to leave Baker Street and take up residence in Queen Anne Street.[1] There had, of course, been earlier signs of strain; and it may well be, considering Holmes's age, that the effects of menopause were the actual cause, if not the overt reason, for that breach between Watson and he.

It is likely, however, that the immediate cause was Holmes's awareness of Watson's burgeoning interest in another lady. To that matter we shall return shortly. For the moment, we will only suggest that it was Holmes, not Watson, who strove to repair the breach.

Watson had long since acquired a taste for Turkish baths; and, by now, Holmes had acquired that taste also. These establishments—"Hammams," as they were called—furnished a means for the sort of physical relaxation that, at his stage of life, Holmes would especially appreciate. Nor did they put his secret into jeopardy. As one passed through the succession of eight hot-air rooms, each hotter than the last,[2] one did so in privacy; and, between times, one was swathed in blankets. All that Watson mentions seeing of Holmes was "a long, thin, nervous arm."[3] Holmes, of course, would take the precaution of declining a massage and, in the Northumberland Avenue establishment, of seeking with

Blanket-swathed clients of a Turkish bath in London, as seen in a rare view from early this century. A cover-up would require little of Sherlock's skill.

Watson that "isolated corner where two couches lie side by side." There, as Watson notes, Holmes became "less reticent and more human than anywhere else"![4]

However, there were limits to the closeness of their relationship, for Watson writes:

> I was nearer to him than anyone else, yet I was always conscious of the great gap between.[5]

With his usual reticence, composed in equal parts of Scottish descent, medical ethics and Victorian prudery, Watson does not elaborate on the nature of that "great gap." Nor did he need to do so, for of course he knew well what it was— the unbridgeable gap of different gender. A man may understand another man, but no man may ever hope fully to understand a woman.

For his part, Holmes recognizes this also. Indeed, he says as much:

> "Woman's heart and mind are insoluble puzzles to the male."[6]

We may note that Holmes at first refuses quite arrogantly to take the illustrious client's case. However, he changes his mind when he is informed by Sir Charles Damery that Baron Adelbert Gruner has "the whole [female] sex at his mercy."[7] That is enough to make Holmes act, even though he is still unaware of the name of his client—his reason for the earlier refusal.

In this case, once again, Holmes is involved in offstage violence and is injured—not, of course, so severely as the newspapers and Watson proclaim, but enough to have blood soaking through the "white linen compress" on his head.[8] According to his account, it was only his skill with the singlestick that saved him from greater injury by his two attackers. However, once again, there was no independent witness and, once again, we have no evidence for the skill which he claims—only the certainty that, whatever happened to his opponent, Holmes himself was injured.

Watson seems seldom surprised by such roughhousing, and in fact refers to "the curious secretive streak in the man that led to many dramatic effects."[9] We suspect the exaggerated version of the assault upon him that Holmes permitted to be published must have had a purpose additional to that stated, one never to be perceived by Watson—to cause him anxiety and bring him back to Holmes's bedside. It was a trick that had worked earlier, as we have seen (p. 49–50); and, of course, it worked again.

Soon Watson was firmly under control—if only for a while. He recognizes the fact, in a phrase that echoes a husband speaking of his dominant wife:

> He gave no explanations and I asked for none. By long experience I had learned the wisdom of obedience.[10]

Yet he did not return to Baker Street; indeed, so far as the Canon reveals, Watson never returned to Baker Street. The partnership had been broken; the breach was to be briefly bridged but was never to be wholly repaired.

The Red Circle

The *Illustrious Client* is considered by Sherlockians as being the last *normal* case in the Canon. All the subsequent cases have had their authenticity—their Canonicity—questioned. For our part, we do not doubt their validity. We believe instead that the perceived changes all result from that widening breach between Holmes and Watson.

In this case, for example, the story is conveyed largely through dialogue. It is as if Watson is no longer so eager to write about Holmes. Certainly there is no fresh information about the great detective. The new tone is well conveyed at the beginning:

> Holmes was accessible upon the side of flattery, and also, to do him justice, upon the side of kindliness.[11]

As Watson contemplates Holmes, he is no longer doing so with the old near-idolatry. This is a cool and unenthusiastic assessment.

Then we have Holmes reading the agony columns of the newspaper and his bitterly cynical commentary:

> "Dear me!" said he, turning over the pages, "what a chorus of groans, cries and bleating.... Here are the *Daily Gazette* extracts of the last fortnight...'Surely Jimmy will not break his mother's heart'—that appears to be irrelevant. 'If the lady who fainted in the Brixton bus'— she does not interest me. 'Every day my heart longs—' Bleat, Watson— unmitigated bleat!"[12]

The earlier phase of kindliness has gone. Now, once again, Holmes is treating the softer emotions with "a gibe and a sneer."[13]

Moreover, as a number of commentators have noted,[14] Watson's account of Holmes's deciphering of the code is so shockingly inaccurate that it makes little sense. Indeed, in reporting this case, Watson's whole attitude is careless—in both senses of that word. He seems to have no personal involvement, either with Holmes or with the case.

This seems to us to solve one of the great mysteries of the Canon, what Dakin has called *The Problem of the Casebook*.[15] The cases recounted in that collection mostly date from the time after the breach between Watson and Holmes. They were written either by an uninterested Watson or by an inept Holmes.

The Blanched Soldier

Here we have the well-known occasion upon which, complains Holmes:

> "...the good Watson...had deserted me for a wife, the only selfish action which I can recall in our association. I was alone."[16]

We can almost hear the whine of self-pity in that final word.

The question of the identity of this Mrs. Watson has long vexed Sherlockian commentators. Was this a second wife, or had the former Mary Morstan returned to Watson's arms after an absence caused, perhaps, by a justifiable jealousy of Holmes? After all, it is not made explicit that Watson's "bereavement"[17] *was* the death of his wife.

For our part, as we have stated (p. 60), we believe that Mary Morstan had died during the interval between the adventures of *The Final Problem* and *The Empty House*. Consequently we are forced to consider seriously the idea that this was a second wife, whose identity can only be a matter for speculation but who was probably much more warmly affectionate than the cool, cerebral Holmes. Certainly such a possibility cannot be discounted.

Yet might it not be that Watson had "deserted" Holmes for someone else's wife, in a temporary liaison that would have been considered too improper to be mentioned at the time when this chronicle was written? Neville St. Clair's wife, perhaps—she who had aroused such poetry of description in Watson, and had kept Holmes sitting sentry all night?[18] This is the view which we favour. We believe that Holmes, when referring to Watson's having deserted him for "a wife," was playing his own game of telling the literal truth, yet deliberately obscuring the real meaning of his words. If Watson had indeed a second wife of his own, that lady gains no least subsequent mention.

This adventure contains that curious reference to "the case which my friend Watson has described as that of the Abbey School, in which the Duke of Greyminster was so deeply involved."[19] Baring-Gould and other commentators have assumed this to be an erroneous citation of the "Adventure of the Priory School," which involved the son of the Duke of Holdernesse. However, in view of Holmes's habit of precision, it seems unlikely that he would make such an error. Greyminster was, as every schoolboy once knew, that great public school of which Hylton Cleaver wrote, or, more accurately, was to write, in the pages of *Chums*. We suggest that the Abbey School was later to be renamed Greyminster School in honour of the Duke—who knows, perhaps as a consequence of that very case to which Holmes was referring?

This is the first case chronicled by Holmes himself. One can imagine the state of mind that forced him into taking up the pen. Once having done so, his opening words do not deal with the task at hand, as one might have expected, but constitute instead a rather merciless, if not downright catty, attack upon "the good Watson:"

The ideas of my friend Watson, though limited, are exceedingly pertinaceous.[20]

Holmes goes on to comment, rather condescendingly:

Speaking of my old friend and biographer, I would take this opportunity to remark that if I burden myself with a companion in my various little inquiries it is not done out of sentiment or caprice, but it is that Watson has some remarkable characteristics of his own, to which in his modesty he has given small attention amid his exaggerated estimates of my own performances.[21]

Furthermore, after a passage in which Holmes justifies his taking pen in hand, he continues his attack:

A confederate who foresees your conclusions and course of action is always dangerous, but one to whom each development comes as a perpetual surprise, and to whom the future is always a closed book, is, indeed, an ideal helpmate.[22]

Earlier commentators have interpreted Holmes's previous sentence, on Watson's qualities, as referring to this lack of prescience. We cannot agree with them since that is a shortcoming, however desirable. The "remarkable characteristics" remain unspecified; indeed, they may have been of a male nature that Holmes was simply not prepared to specify! Instead, throughout the opening scenes of this case, Watson is again and again chastised; yet it is readily apparent to the reader that Holmes is unable to recount the tale without invoking his erstwhile companion. It is as if he were attempting to authenticate the manner of telling. However, finally Homes makes the astounding admission:

…and here it is that I miss my Watson.[23]

Note that revealing phrase; "*my* Watson." Despite all the derision he has poured upon poor Watson's inadequacies, Holmes shows his genuine and possessive feeling in this one aside.

Dakin, once again, has noted something strange about the style of this story,[24] but once again has come to an erroneous conclusion: that the narrator is some person other than Holmes (or Watson). We suggest instead that we are hearing the authentic voice of Holmes—and a jealous Holmes at that! It is a curious combination of self-justification and injured protest with praise and insult for his erstwhile companion.

For our part, we consider that those "remarkable characteristics" which Holmes mentioned are qualities—or abilities!—that Holmes would have been quite unable to particularize without revealing his own femininity.

The Three Gables

Although Watson's second wife—if wife indeed she was—does not gain direct mention in this adventure, it is clear that he is not living at Baker Street, for he comments:

> I had not seen Holmes for some days.[25]

This adventure contains that extraordinarily revealing passage in which Holmes, for a moment, quite forgets his assumed masculinity:

> Holmes clapped his hand to his pocket.
> "Lookin' for your gun, Massa Holmes?"
> "No; for my scent-bottle, Steve."[26]

As we have remarked earlier (p. 4), who ever heard of a Victorian man carrying a scent-bottle? There are other indications also. Holmes's praise of Douglas Maberley, for example, has a tone much more that of a woman for a man than of a man for another man:

> "What a magnificent creature he was! One could not connect death with such a man. I have never known anyone so vitally alive. He lived intensely—every fibre of him!"[27]

After this appreciation, the dead Douglas's mother says:

> "You remember him as he was—debonair and splendid. You did not see the moody, morose, brooding creature into which he developed. His heart was broken. In a single month I seemed to see my gallant boy turn into a worn-out cynical man."

Sherlock losing a duel of words with a dangerous woman. Isadora Klein has perceived the truth—and is using it to her advantage. (The Three Gables)

Instantly Holmes responds:

"A love affair—a woman?"[28]

It is unlikely that a man would have perceived so instantly the cause of young Maberley's decline and death. Furthermore, a man might have been reluctant to ask so pointed a question of a mother concerning her son's seduction.

Indeed, this adventure epitomises the developing sexuality apparent in those later chronicles collected in *The Casebook of Sherlock Holmes*. Such frank discussion would have been unthinkable in the earlier chronicles.

To give another example in support of this thesis, let us consider the character who masquerades under the name of a Cumberland mountain, Langdale Pike. "This strange, languid creature," as Watson calls him,[29] is quite plainly a homosexual—and may indeed have been a portrait of the unfortunate and notorious Oscar Wilde himself:

> Langdale was [Holmes's] human book of reference upon all matters of social scandal.... [He] spent his waking hours in the bow window of a St. James' Street club, and was the receiving-station, as well as the transmitter, for all the gossip of the Metropolis. He made, it was said, a four-figure income by the paragraphs which he contributed every week to the garbage papers which cater for an inquisitive public. If ever, far down in the turbid depths of London life, there was some strange swirl or eddy, it was marked with automatic exactness by this human dial upon the surface.[30]

Watson's distaste cannot be disguised; but then, Watson was a very masculine man.

The perception of homosexuality is stressed by the reiteration by Holmes, in the dialogue recorded by Watson, of that word so frequently and so unkindly applied at the turn of the century. When the police inspector observes:

> "Seems to be the end of some queer novel."

Holmes responds with irony:

> "It may certainly prove to be the end of a queer tale."[31]

Soon afterwards, he is observing:

> "It seems a queer thing to break into a house."[32]

and later he speaks smilingly of "Queer grammar."[33]

This chronicle again makes evident the fact that Holmes is regretting Watson's departure. This is revealed in an unexpected fashion. When the Three Gables has been burgled, Holmes admits to Watson:

> "I made a mistake, I fear, in not asking you to spend the night on guard."[34]

Note that Holmes seems not even to have considered being the guard himself, but has instead assigned the task to one man, the lawyer Sutro, and is regretting not having allotted it to another. Yet Holmes had no other urgent tasks on hand. Once again, we are given reason to doubt his oft-vaunted fighting abilities. Had he by then abandoned the pretence, at least to Watson? Or was Holmes possibly in an unusually frail condition at this time? We must wait a few months, and see!

A more subtle indication is given in Holmes's interchanges with the ruthless, but beautiful and extremely feminine Isadora Klein. Evidently she has immediately perceived the truth about Holmes. With teasing bitchiness, she proceeds to mock him—while, at the same time, striving to bend him to her purposes:

> "Come and sit down, gentlemen. Let us talk this matter over. I feel I may be frank with you, Mr. Holmes. You have the feelings of a gentleman. How quick a woman's instinct is to find it out. I will treat you as a friend."[35]

Watson is ignored and, typically, fails to perceive the sardonic overtones in Isadora's words. After Holmes's brusque response, she continues the assault:

> "No doubt it was foolish of me to threaten a brave man like yourself."[36]

During the duel of words that follows, she continues to play a game of double meanings. She is speaking apparently of her minions, but actually to Holmes, when she says:

> "They are good hounds who run silent."

Holmes comprehends this and responds:

> "Such hounds have a way sooner or later of biting the hand that feeds them."[37]

Moreover, when Isadora states firmly:

> "They will take what comes to them. That is what they are paid for. I shall not appear in the matter."[38]

Holmes continues to reject these implicit overtures, despite her further hints, responding:

"Unless I bring you into it."
"No, no; you would not. You are a gentleman. It is a woman's secret."[39]

As the interplay between them continues, Watson observes a little of what is happening without understanding it, for he notes:

She broke into a ripple of laughter.... So roguish and exquisite did she look as she stood before us with a challenging smile that I felt of all Holmes' criminals this was the one whom he would find it hardest to face.[40]

However, Holmes continues to reject her overtures. She tries one more time, at once appealing and—as Holmes surely realizes—threatening:

"But you must look at it with my eyes, Mr. Holmes. You must realize it from the point of view of a woman who sees all her life's ambition about to be ruined at the last moment. Is a woman to be blamed if she protects herself?"[41]

Nor does she fail. Isadora is not subjected to prosecution for the crimes she has committed and instigated, nor does she lose her titled fiancee. All that she is forced to do by Holmes is to pay a financial forfeit that, to so rich a woman, is quite trivial. Watson was right; this was a criminal with whom Holmes was unable to deal effectively.

There is an echo here of that other, infinitely less evil woman whom Holmes had encountered in the "Scandal in Bohemia"—and who had likewise perceived his femininity, his Achilles' heel.

The Mazarin Stone

This case, with its peculiar provenance, has been perhaps the most questioned in the Canon. The unnamed (and unknown) third-person narrator seems at times to have rearranged much of the familiar set-up at 221B Baker Street—to such a degree, indeed, that the very authenticity of the chronicle has been brought into serious question.

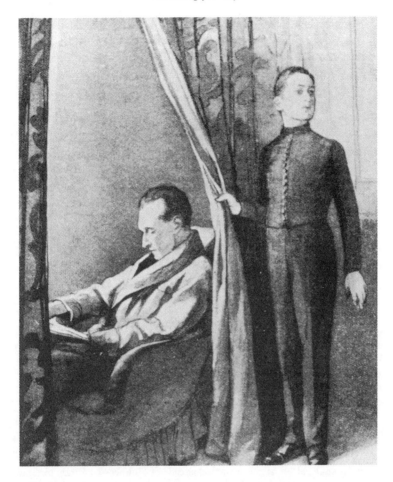

Billy the page and Sherlock. Though the Holmes of this scene is a dummy, the similarity in profile is striking. (The Mazarin Stone)

There is, however, no error in the portrayal of Holmes, not the slightest doubt that here we have a true depiction of the Master. His words, his behaviour are authentic to the utmost degree. Ellery Queen to the contrary, the formula for writing an adventure of Sherlock Holmes is not "an easy one." We may be assured that whoever the writer may have been—the absurd suggestion that it was Mrs. Mary Watson can, we feel, be dismissed out of hand—that person knew Holmes and knew him very well indeed.

We are inclined to agree with those perceptive commentators who have identified Mycroft Holmes as the chronicler of this adventure. It is pleasant to speculate upon what circumstance might have prompted that corpulent relaxation-worshipper to take up his pen. Might it have been at Sherlock's own request, to show Watson that he was not essential?

When Watson, still living away from Baker Street—though, again, no second Mrs. Watson gains mention—goes to visit Holmes at the outset of this adventure, he finds his friend in bed, even though it is by then "seven in the evening of a lovely summer's day."[42] He encounters Billy the page and is told that Holmes has been working in disguise:

> "To-day he was an old woman. Fairly took me in, he did, and I ought to know his ways by now."[43]

In his career as recorded by Watson, Holmes disguised himself no less than thirteen times as a man (or fourteen, if we include his long-running impersonation of Sherlock Holmes, the man), but only once as a woman. The success of that one performance may be judged by the fact that despite Holmes's 'disguise' as an old (!) woman, Count Negretto Sylvius was impressed enough to retrieve the dropped parasol.[44]

Is it possible that Billy, without being aware of it, was seeing Holmes *without* his disguise? This theory is supported by Holmes's later, wry comment:

> "You've seen me as an old lady, Watson. I was never more convincing."[45]

Within moments of Watson's encounter with Billy, a pale and drawn Holmes is with them. Watson has been warned already of Holmes's condition by Billy, who is frightened for his employer's health: "He just gets paler and thinner," he has told Watson, "and he eats nothing."[46]

Since Holmes was fit and well at the time of the Three Gables affair only a few months earlier, there has indeed been some change in his physical condition. A pregnancy at the age of forty-nine, however terminated, is certain to prove a most demanding ordeal. In the stages before that termination, Holmes would have been especially inclined to lean upon Watson for support (see p. 54), whether or not Watson had been recently his lover.

Probably the strain of his experience, so late in Holmes's life, answers another question: why the Great Detective chose to retire, while still at the height of his reasoning powers. Only one adventure interposes between this case, when Holmes's poor physical condition is so much stressed, and that premature departure to the peaceful surroundings of the Sussex Downs. Surely it is reasonable to deduce that, despite a temporary rallying, Holmes's health was so adversely affected by this late pregnancy that a long convalescence was forced on him?

A striking feature of this adventure is the anxiety displayed by Holmes concerning young Billy, the page. After he has gazed unwisely out of the window when Count Sylvius is in the offing, Holmes springs into action to save him from possible danger:

> "That will do, Billy," said he. "You were in danger of your life then, my boy, and I can't do without you just yet."[47]

Shortly afterward he is saying to Watson:

> "That boy is a problem, Watson. How far am I justified in allowing him to be in danger?"[48]

The parental tone in that "my boy," and Holmes's unwonted approach to Watson for advice, each reinforce the idea that Billy may have been their son; and this is a question that needs to be examined.

How old was Billy? Well, at a time when long stays at school were not enforced by statute, he may have been as young as twelve or as old as about sixteen or seventeen, though a lesser age seems likely. On that basis, it is certainly possible that he was Holmes's child, either (if he were around sixteen) of that first pregnancy, terminated in France in 1887 (see pp. 21–22) or, if he were only around twelve, of the more recent one that precipitated the Great Hiatus (see p. 79).

Very well, then, it is conceivable; but we believe it is in the highest degree unlikely. First of all, we do not consider that Watson was, in either instance, the father; all evidence is to the contrary (see pp. 22 and 56). Secondly, we do not consider Holmes to have been the sort of sentimental mother likely, after relinquishing her child, to desire suddenly to have him back. Finally and most cogently, Billy is (as portrayed in the chronicles) an extremely English youth of what would then be styled "the lower classes." He gives no least suggestion of a French upbringing—and any child of Holmes would surely either have been reared in France or, if in England, at a higher social level. All in all, this is an idea that we cannot favour.

Instead, we believe that Holmes had come to regard Billy as a son because of the help and support received during those difficult months. Billy had become in some measure a substitute for the child that Holmes was unable to bear—or, if a living child *was* born in France, to rear. Yet, whatever Holmes's regard for him, Billy cannot have responded to it. He must shortly afterward have left Baker Street, for he gains no mention in the three remaining chronicles.

No, Watson was not Billy's father, nor was Holmes his mother. It is a great deal more likely, however, that Watson was the cause of Holmes's pregnancy— even though Watson might by then have been again married to another. We may note that, in responding to Watson's offer of help and claim that he has "nothing to do for a day or two," Holmes replies:

> "Your morals don't improve, Watson. You have added fibbing to your other vices."[49]

We believe he was not only referring to the impropriety of a married man— and a busy doctor, at that—spending time with another woman (himself) but also commenting caustically upon the cause of his own physical problems! Nevertheless, it is clear that Watson has been forgiven, that the offer of a time together has been accepted; for, at the very end of the adventure, Holmes instructs Billy to:

> "…tell Mrs. Hudson that I should be glad if she would send up dinner for two as soon as possible."[50]

The Creeping Man

The second paragraph of this chronicle makes it all too clear that the reconciliation between Holmes and Watson, if reconciliation there was, came to a quick end. Watson writes:

> It was one Sunday evening early in September of the year 1903 that I received one of Holmes's laconic messages: "Come at one if convenient—if inconvenient come all the same.—S.H." The relations between us in those latter days were peculiar. He was a man of habits, narrow and concentrated habits, and I had become one of them. As an institution I was like the violin, the shag tobacco, the old black pipe, the index books, and others perhaps less excusable. When it was a case of active work and a comrade was needed upon whose nerve he could

place some reliance, my role was obvious. But apart from this I had uses. I was a whetstone for his mind. I stimulated him. He liked to think aloud in my presence. His remarks could hardly be said to be made to me—many of them would have been as appropriately addressed to his bedstead—but nonetheless, having formed the habit, it had become in some way helpful that I should register and interject. If I irritated him by a certain methodical slowness in my mentality, that irritation served only to make his own flame-like intuitions and impressions flash up the more vividly and swiftly. Such was my humble role in our alliance.[51]

In this unique catalogue of complaint, this psalm of self-pity, there is so much to comment upon that one scarcely knows where to begin. Moreover, its tone is echoed in a later paragraph stressing that Watson had not returned to the fireside of 221B Baker Street, when he states plaintively that Holmes greeted him back "to what had once been my home."[52]

Even the most casual reader would find it difficult to overlook the wistful regret of this phrasing. Evidently Watson's recent relationship, be it with another man's wife or with a second wife of his own, has ended quickly and unhappily—temporarily or permanently—and he is wishing that things were again as they had once been with Holmes.

Watson feels as if he has been left behind, now that Holmes's life is flowing into new channels. He perceives now that he is being viewed merely as one of the props of Holmes's past life—as something hard to discard, but no longer either of service or of great value. When Watson grumbles that Holmes speaks to him as if he were speaking to his bedstead, the implications are surely obvious.

Yet Holmes's femininity is now asserting itself more strongly. The cold mental processes that had formerly characterized him are being replaced by "flame-like intuitions and impressions."

It is noticeable also that Holmes is no longer vaunting, to Watson at least, his physical prowess; Watson, by now, knows better. Instead, when there is need for strength, Holmes unhesitatingly calls upon Watson, even though they are not seeing one another regularly.

Though Watson is loyally responding to these appeals, he is doing so rather resentfully. The old, good relationship has ended; he admits that the new one is "peculiar" and clearly gains little satisfaction from it. His comrade of former days is turning into a new and different person, with whom Watson no longer feels at ease. As a physician, no doubt he understands in theory the consequences of a late, unhappily terminated pregnancy and of menopause. As a man, however, he is finding their effects hard to accept.

Moreover, Holmes is now prone to phases of surprising indecisiveness. He and Watson take their luggage with them to Camford and leave it at the hotel—The Chequers, an inn which Holmes has noted with feminine percipience as offering "linen [that] was above reproach."[53] Clearly this indicates a planned overnight stay. However, once he has talked to Professor Presbury and learned of the curiously-named Dorak, Holmes says to the Professor's assistant:

> "We return to London this afternoon, Mr. Bennett."[54]

They do not do so. Instead, walking "hotelwards," Holmes pauses at a post office and sends a telegram. He and Watson await the reply at the hotel; predictably enough, it does not arrive until evening.[55] It contains nothing that would enforce a longer stay in Camford; yet, while ensconced in the hotel's sitting-room, Holmes states calmly:

> "I should not expect any fresh developments until next Tuesday. In the meantime we can only…enjoy the amenities of this charming town."[56]

By morning, however, he has changed his mind once again:

> "I am a busy man, and Dr. Watson has his patients to attend to."[57]

So back to London they go!

These are clear evidences of vacillation. No reasonable hypothesis can give logic to such an on-again, off-again sequence.

There is a particular interest, perhaps, in the person to whom the telegram was addressed. He is a man unknown to Watson:

> "Mercer is since your time," said Holmes. "He is my general utility man who looks up routine business. It was important to know something of the man with whom our Professor was so secretly corresponding. His nationality connects up with the Prague visit."[58]

This over-explanation—for Holmes was emphatically *not* given to such detailed self-accountings—provokes a dry response from Watson, who for once is not fooled:

"Thank goodness that something connects with something."[59]

All in all it is evident, as Watson states with unwitting percipience, that their relationship is by then in its "latter days."[60] Though it seems never to have been quite brought to an end, it was never to regain its former warmth and closeness, at least during the period covered by the chronicles. Things were changing, and Holmes was recognizing this fact:

"When one tries to rise above Nature, one is liable to fall below it. The highest type of man may revert to the animal if he leaves the straight road of destiny."[61]

Though this is overtly a comment upon Professor Presbury's strivings to contravert natural processes by attempting to rejuvenate himself. However, we believe it is much more than that. Surely we may interpret this as a personal statement, an admission that, in taking the path he had chosen, Holmes had been striving against *his own* nature, only to be ultimately conquered by it. He was recognizing reluctantly that, as he grew older, his "animal nature"—his sexuality—was overwhelming him and driving him away from the path of his choice. The part he had played for so long was becoming increasingly difficult to sustain while he remained in the full, harsh light of public view. It was becoming necessary to retire to a quieter place and to play that part less often, before a less demanding audience. He admits the fact:

"It's surely time that I disappeared into that little farm of my dreams."[62]

Holmes Alone

The Lion's Mane

THIS TALE IS ONE OF THE TWO penned by Holmes himself. As one might predict, it contains an early reference to Watson's whereabouts:

> "The good Watson had passed almost beyond my ken."

and goes on to the startling revelation that "an occasional weekend visit was the most that I ever saw of him."[1]

This isolation from Watson was to span a decade, from the end of 1903 until the autumn of 1914.

Indeed, Watson seems for a time to have been supplanted in Holmes's affections; first of all, perhaps, by Mercer of *The Creeping Man* and later, somewhat mysteriously, by a neighbour of Holmes, one Harold Stackhurst:

> He and I were always friendly from the day I came to the coast, and he was the one man who was on such terms with me that we could drop in on each other in the evenings without an invitation.[2]

This unheard-of familiarity must have been occasioned by some other attractions of the fortunate Mr. Stackhurst than the mere fact that he was a sportsman, having been "a well-known rowing blue in his day."[3] Holmes was woefully ignorant of most popular sports, as we have shown, and it seems unlikely that he would have desired to spend much time sitting at the feet of a man who kept saying: "And then I won...."

True enough, Harold Stackhurst was "an excellent all-round scholar." Yet the scholarship of any gentleman who ran a coaching establishment in such an out-of-the-way part of the country was not likely, in itself, to impress a person who had lived so long in London—certainly not sufficient to impress so widely knowledgeable a person as Sherlock Holmes. No; we believe there was a quite different attraction!

Whatever the intensity of the relationship between the two, it is clear that Holmes, despite his retirement and despite Doctor Watson (or would it be more correct to say 'to spite Doctor Watson'?), was enjoying a different sort of male company.

Was it a coincidence that Holmes had chosen to live in a lonely cottage, close only to Stackhurst's coaching establishment? Might there be a piece of oblique concealment in Holmes's comment noted above, that the friendship began when he came to the coast? Though this suggests that Holmes and Stackhurst met at that time, it does not quite say so. Is it possible, instead, that they met first in London and that Holmes had chosen his cottage because of its propinquity to the Stackhurst establishment, with an aim of improving a mere acquaintance into something much closer?

Might this, indeed, have been the real reason for Holmes's earlier-expressed longing to disappear to that "little farm of my dreams"?[4] Perhaps the bees were not quite so important as Watson had been led to believe!

This adventure contains another of those oblique admissions by Holmes of his femininity. He states:

> "Women have seldom been an attraction to me, for my brain has always governed my heart."[5]

After this deliberate verbal smokescreen—it may even be read, perhaps, as a reference to the homosexual temptations to which he had preserved himself from succumbing—Holmes goes on to comment on the attractions of Miss Maude Bellamy, stating that:

> "...no young man would cross her path unscathed."[6]

If she were indeed so very attractive, then any older man of normal proclivities would also have responded in some measure to her feminine charms. Not so Holmes; but then, as we know by now, Holmes was by nature immune.

Yet in other respects, this adventure underlines how greatly Holmes was changing. Notice the sensuous, heavily sexual overtones in his description of the Lion's Mane:

> "…a curious waving, vibrating, hairy creature with streaks of silver among
> its yellow tresses. It pulsated with a slow, heavy dilation and contraction."[7]

Holmes seems to have been simultaneously attracted and repelled, proceeding to destroy the creature with the unnecessary speed of one hastening to excise a temptation from the mind. This would have been a very Victorian reaction. Was that not a period when the legs of tables were covered, when locomotives were inside-connected so that the in-and-out motion of the pistons could not be observed, and when even the wheels of tram-cars (streetcars) were covered by "decency-boards"? That Holmes should have conveyed such a sexual image in his writing shows the change wrought by menopause.

In the earlier adventures Holmes had repeatedly emphasized his selectivity in study and the acquisition of knowledge. Now he admits:

> I am an omnivorous reader with a strangely retentive memory
> for trifles.[8]

and states elsewhere that:

> I hold a vast store of out-of-the-way knowledge, without scientific
> system…my mind is like a crowded box-room with packets of all sorts
> stowed away therein—so many that I may well have but a vague
> perception of what was there.[9]

Contrast this with Holmes's own statement, just before the earliest of the cases in which Watson shared:

> "…I consider that a man's brain originally is like a little empty attic,
> and you have to stock it with such furniture as you choose. A fool takes
> in all the lumber of every sort that he comes across, so that the knowledge

which might be useful to him gets crowded out, or at best is jumbled up with a lot of other things, so that he has a difficulty in laying his hands upon it. Now the skilled workman is very careful indeed as to what he takes into his brain-attic. He will have nothing but the tools which may help him in doing his work, but of these he has a large assortment, and all in the most perfect order. It is a mistake to think that that little room has elastic walls and can distend to any extent. Depend upon it there comes a time when for every addition of knowledge you forget something that you knew before. It is of the highest importance, therefore, not to have useless facts elbowing out the useful ones."[10]

Could any two attitudes be more contradictory?

As Nathan L. Bengis has pointed out,[11] Holmes made a hash of this case in its earliest stages and contrived to recover himself only after the Lion's Mane had almost claimed a second victim. Yes, Holmes may have had enlarged photographs made of the wounds of Fitzroy McPherson,[12] in properly scientific fashion; yet why did he not realize immediately, from the condition of McPherson's hair and his Burberry overcoat, that he had been in the water?[13] The earlier Holmes would never have missed so obvious a point.

It is likely enough that, had Watson been the chronicler, he might well have stressed Holmes's "eventual triumph against every difficulty,"[14] glossing over those failures. But the cold-minded Holmes, *soi-disant*, wished—or so he proclaimed—to expound his cases as examples of pure reasoning. Instead, when writing up this case, he takes pride in quoting the words of praise or admiration uttered about himself by the participants and quite glosses over this fundamental failure. He admits only that he was "slow at the outset—culpably slow"—and proceeds to offer excuses.[15]

Holmes's decline is made sadly obvious in this case—and it is even sadder that he is himself unaware of it. Instead, he is revelling in the adulation of persons to whom, in earlier days, he would scarcely have paid attention.

Another mystery of this story is the identity of the person or persons whom Holmes was addressing when he wrote:

"You will know, or Watson has written in vain…"[16]

This unexpected lapse into the second-person mode of address is perhaps equalled by Watson's earlier threat at the time of The Veiled Lodger, to reveal "the whole story concerning the politician, the lighthouse and the trained cormorant." On that occasion, Watson noted pointedly:

"There is at least one reader who will understand."[17]

That reader was never to be identified in the Canon; nor has his or her identity been determined by Sherlockian scholars. Was Holmes addressing that same reader, or is there a second mystery here?

His Last Bow

For this adventure Holmes takes on a new masculine disguise, as Altamont the Irish-American. For this purpose, he sports a "small goatee beard" giving him "a general resemblance to the caricatures of Uncle Sam."[18] We have no reason to suppose this a natural growth; such beards could be acquired from any theatrical costumier.

After a long interval—presumably those occasional weekend visits had long since come to an end—Watson is here reunited with Holmes, however briefly. This causes him considerable joy:

"I feel twenty years younger, Holmes. I have seldom felt so happy as when I got your wire asking me to meet you at Harwich with the car."[19]

As for Holmes, it is clear that he is equally delighted:

"I've hardly seen you in the light yet. How have the years used you? You look the same blithe boy as ever."[20]

As S.C. Roberts has commented, this is "A remarkable tribute to an old campaigner of sixty-two."[21] Quite evidently, in his pleasure, Holmes was regarding his old companion through the most brightly tinted of rose-coloured spectacles! This is our last chronicled encounter with them, on the eve of the Great War. The only hint of the future is given in a mysterious comment from Holmes:

"As to you, Watson, you are joining us with your old service, as I understand, so London won't be out of your way."[22]

Roberts points out that Watson's age would preclude any normal military service and speculates that he might have been taken onto the staff of a military hospital.[23] But surely, if so, Holmes would not have said "joining us"?

The geography of this case becomes relevant here. We find astonishing Baring-Gould's ready acceptance of Gordon Sewell's suggestion, that von Bork's house was on the south coast of England.[24] The house was within view of Harwich[25] and was thus quite certainly in northernmost Essex or southernmost Suffolk—thus, on the east coast. Moreover, von Bork's wife and household had left for Flushing[26]—a port of The Netherlands and a very probable destination from Harwich, but a highly inconvenient and improbable one if the von Borks had indeed been living on the south coast.

Very well, then, von Bork lived on the east coast and Watson would be travelling thence, through or close by London, to his unstated destination and "his old service." We suggest that he was travelling either to Aldershot or to a camp on Salisbury Plain, in order to rejoin the army. We suggest also that he had either secured an exemption allowing him to enlist in a regular capacity, despite his age, or, more probably, that he was to be joining a Department in which age was not an important consideration—a Department to which Holmes himself was also attached. Indeed, it is conceivable that Holmes had again (as in the instance of the purchase of Watson's medical practice) operated through others, in order to ensure that his old comrade would once more be close at hand.

It seems evident that a reunion of Watson and Holmes was in prospect for their declining years and that, when Holmes said:

"Good old Watson! You are the one fixed point in a changing age."[27]

he was revelling in the anticipation of that reunion.

What had happened to Harold Stackhurst, we shall probably never know; but it is surely clear that Holmes had been unhappily enduring loneliness in his years of retirement. Knowing what we do about the great detective, we may perceive this from the very title he chose for what he styles the *magnum opus* of his latter years—his *Practical Handbook of Bee Culture, with some Observations upon the Segregation of the Queen.*[28] That second clause is ponderous and unnecessary for a work of wide scope, especially from the author of such succinctly titled works as *The Book of Life,*[29] *Upon The Distinction Between the Ashes of the Various Tobaccos*[30] and the *Polyphonic Motets of Lassus.*[31] No, this was yet another of the tantalizing hints Holmes gave to an impercipient audience; and, on this occasion, with an element of sadness, even bitterness.

It is good to know that there was to be, for Holmes, this reunion with the beloved Watson—that the years alone were at an end.

Through Other Eyes

IN THE COURSE OF OUR EXAMINATION of the evidence presented in the individual cases of Sherlock Holmes, we have made mention of a number of observations by earlier commentators. However, now we have completed that examination we feel it desirable to examine some of their conclusions in more detail.

Among the very large number of works in which the Holmesian saga has been annotated or commented upon—the recent bibliographies assembled by De Waal[1] are quite staggering in coverage—relatively few make any attempt to examine the sexual elements in the relationship between Holmes and Watson. Interestingly enough, this relationship has been much more thoroughly explored in cartoons (appearing in such magazines as *Playboy* and in some of the lighter-hearted journals of Sherlockian societies) than in texts.

There have, it is true, been some works in which Holmes's sexual proclivities have received extended treatment, but these in their varying ways are all very far from being works of scholarship. At one extreme, they include Nicholas Meyer's portrait of a very improbable and uncanonical Holmes as an early patient of Sigmund Freud[2]—a portrait perhaps even less palatable in the book than in the film version. Towards the other extreme is Billy Wilder's classic film *The Private Life of Sherlock Holmes*,[3] with its oblique implications of a homosexual relationship; while quite at that other extreme is *The Sexual Adventures of Sherlock Holmes*,[4] an overtly pornographic work which does not even pretend to represent the real Holmes. Rex Stout's tongue-in-cheek suggestion that Watson was a woman[5] has received a surprising degree of consideration and even some measure of endorsement (from Virginia Johnson, at least[6]). However, there have also been many spirited refutations.[7] We are in entire accord with this latter opinion. The evidences for Watson's masculinity are to be found in so many adventures that we find no need to consider the matter further.

Of the remaining works in which the Holmes/Watson relationship is examined, most do so only briefly or obliquely. The exception is Christopher Redmond's study *In Bed With Sherlock Holmes* (1974). In this work, surprisingly, only the most passing attention is paid to the possibility—we would say, the virtual certainty—that Holmes was a woman; instead, it is dismissed as merely a joke of Sherlockians.[8] Since Redmond was aware of our earlier brief study—indeed, he cites it in his bibliography—we can only regret that it did not impress him. We must trust that this fuller treatment of the question will prove more convincing to him.

Nevertheless, several points noted by Redmond are of interest here. There is his comment on Watson, for example:

> Of Watson, the reader gets a clear impression, not only from *The Sign of the Four*, but from all the other tales: and one of the chief elements of the picture is that Watson is fond of the opposite sex, particularly in contrast with the ascetic, almost asexual Holmes.[9]

This, of course, was Holmes's problem—his extreme unease with sex, the cause as well as the inevitable consequence of the lifelong game of impersonation that he played. When Watson was for so long not even aware that Holmes was a woman, and when Holmes was reluctant to admit even this closest of his friends behind the mask that he wore, how could he compete with the charming and very feminine Miss Morstan? Is it surprising that, while still feeling the need for Watson's masculine company, Holmes went to such lengths to avoid encountering the woman who had usurped him? Redmond likewise perceives the continuing problem that Holmes faced, without understanding its true nature:

> Watson's eye for the ladies, specifically for the pretty ones, is made apparent in story after story.... He looks at pretty women; he looks at them, when he can arrange it, with the light behind them, the better to get an eyeful of what he modestly calls in several places the "figure." Indeed, that is the key word in Watson's description of women.[10]

And there is poor Holmes, lean and small-breasted, with nothing but intellect with which to try to charm Watson! Though, as we believe, he succeeded for a while, it was only to lose Watson again within a few more years to another lady's attractions. We must take comfort in the hint in *His Last Bow* that, with the waning of Watson's own sexual urges and the changes in Holmes, there may have come a final and lasting reunion.

Redmond perceives also, without understanding its cause, Holmes's special sympathy with women. He notes that Holmes is "infallibly kind when a woman needs kindness"[11] and that he "listens to women and goes far out of his way to deal with their concerns, making efforts he probably would not make for men."[12] In contrast, Redmond is puzzled by the apparent hostility of Holmes to emotions and to the thought of marriage, for he comments:

> In story after story, Holmes is made to deny, to protest perhaps too much, that he could have an emotional interest in the opposite sex.[13]

The real problems lie, of course, in Redmond's presumption of the nature of that "opposite sex" and his consequent failure to realize that Holmes could never marry a woman! This misinterpretation is evident when Redmond quotes Watson's words on Holmes:

> …he had a remarkable gentleness and courtesy in his dealings with women. He disliked and distrusted the sex, but he was always a chivalrous opponent.[14]

Redmond comments: "Perhaps 'opponent' is indeed the key word."[15] We would suggest instead that, because Watson as well as Redmond misunderstood the situation (Watson, at least, would be enlightened later!), the proper word was "proponent." In similar fashion, other commentators have perceived part of the truth, without comprehending it. In particular, Ian McQueen's searching and scholarly analysis contains several valuable insights. He notes the problem of Holmes's health:

> To put it briefly, Holmes seems to have deteriorated rapidly after the Return, yet in *The Hound of the Baskervilles* he was apparently perfectly well…. Notwithstanding Watson's assertion in *Black Peter*, an 1895 case, that Holmes had never been 'in better form, both mental and physical,' the position had dramatically changed for the worse two years

The stance before the fire is determinedly masculine—but see how the folds of the trousers reveal the shape of Sherlock's legs! (A Scandal in Bohemia)

later. His iron constitution showed symptoms of giving way and his holiday in Cornwall in *The Devil's Foot* was taken on the orders of a Harley Street doctor so that he might 'surrender to complete rest' in an effort 'to avert a complete breakdown.' Though under fifty years of age, Holmes was far from well. The illness, though what it was is not disclosed, may have caused Holmes discomfort or pain, which would explain why he became so bad-tempered on occasion.

By 1902, as Watson explained in *The Three Garridebs*, it was [Holmes's] habit to spend several days in bed from time to time, and he retired soon afterwards, when still only about fifty years old. A voluntary retirement at that age hardly sounds consonant with the true character of Holmes, a man so completely engulfed in the affairs of his specially chosen profession. An enforced retirement on medical advice may have been unavoidable.[16]

This reading of the evidence from the adventures fits in exactly with ours; and, of course, we have presented our interpretation of it.

McQueen's deductions concerning the relationship between John and Mary Watson after their marriage are also of great interest. He notes those lengthy intramarital separations—the two spring weeks in *The Copper Beeches*, the adventurings with Holmes in *The Cardboard Box*, and the long continental journey in *The Final Problem* (which McQueen computes as occupying ten days at absolute minimum).[17] Though we do not accept McQueen's date—August, 1890—for the second of these cases (see pp. 159–160), we accept his general thesis. McQueen also stresses the unsatisfactory nature of Watson's practice and, significantly, wonders:

> Was Holmes unaware of the doctor's domestic situation? Or had he tactfully kept away for fear of embarrassment?[18]

As we have seen, indeed he had!

McQueen's ensuing analysis is also significant:

> There may be a common answer to all these questions; that the relationship between Watson and his wife had steadily deteriorated and she had finally left him. The parting would in all probability have made Watson careless of his medical duties. He had 'another set of vices' beyond the peccadilloes he had confessed to Holmes at the time of

their first meeting in *A Study in Scarlet*. Gambling was one of them. He was to admit somewhat ruefully in *Shoscombe Old Place* that he had paid for racing 'with about half my wound pension.' He must have been a difficult man to live with. Even Holmes, who was not exactly faultless himself, was heard to complain, in *The Three Students*, of the doctor's 'eternal tobacco' and 'irregularity of meals.' At times of mental pressure and stress Watson's propensities for gambling and drink probably came to the fore, though whether they contributed to the broken marriage or were resorted to by Watson in his loneliness is unknown.

We suspect that Watson was probably cruel, perhaps even violent at times, to Mary, especially when he was in drink. It was a family failing. *The Sign of Four* begins with a deductive demonstration by Holmes, when he described the doctor's 'unhappy brother' by reference of an examination to his watch. 'He was a man of untidy habits—very untidy and careless. He was left with good prospects, but he threw away his chances, lived for some time in poverty with occasional short intervals of prosperity, and, finally, taking to drink, he died.' So Holmes summed up his findings, which Watson confirmed were 'absolutely correct in every particular'. Is it not reasonably likely that Watson had also succumbed to a similar, but fortunately not fatal, downfall? He had good prospects in the medical profession, periods of poverty through idleness and betting, intervals of prosperity when he troubled to work hard in his practice, and was at all times liable to take excesses of alcohol. He needed Beaune, for example, to stimulate him to tackle Holmes about the latter's drug-taking on the afternoon Miss Morstan arrived with her pearls. He may have become more and more reliant upon the bottle as his marriage started to break down....

The breakdown of Watson's marriage may not have been entirely his fault. With his great 'experience of women which extends over many nations and three separate continents', Watson may have found the former governess too frigid a female for his sexual palate and have sought solace elsewhere. But whatever the prime cause may have been, the marriage failed, and Watson's once flourishing practice declined.[19]

As has been made evident earlier, we entirely endorse McQueen's deduction that Watson's marriage had a rocky course. However, we are less inclined to blame this either on drugs and drink or on Watson's philandering. Instead, we suspect that Holmes was the rock upon which the marriage went aground and, perhaps, was ultimately wrecked. If McQueen is right in suspecting that Mary was sexually frigid, it might well have made Holmes seem a more appealing alternative; but we do not believe that was the problem. Instead, we conclude that Holmes's attraction was essentially intellectual. The combination of sex and high intellect can be more appealing to a man than sex unallied with intelligence—at least in the long run. Concerning the bereavement mentioned in *The Empty House*, McQueen seems to accept that this was Mary Watson's death;[20] but Christopher Morley speculated instead that it was their separation.[21] We have set forth our own conclusions already (see p. 87). McQueen comments:

> We can only be sorry for Watson that a marriage that began with such happy promise should have ended in tragedy.[22]

We wonder, though, who else could have had the good fortune to be consoled by Sherlock Holmes?

Gavin Brend, who analyzes at length the problems presented by the references in the chronicles to John Watson's marriages, was struck by the fact that Mary Watson contrived always to be out of the way when her husband was called on by Sherlock Holmes. Brend notes that Watson referred to the "accommodating neighbour" who would take over his medical practice whenever needful, and suggests that Watson should also have paid tribute to his "accommodating wife."[23]

Whilst we concur that Mary Watson, no doubt because of her gratitude to Holmes, was apparently quite willing that her husband should join in his investigations, we have noted also that Holmes took particular pains to avoid Mrs. Watson. Watson's availability was not always through Mary's goodwill; it was also a result of Holmes's skilled timing of his visits.

Although so attractive and so feminine, Mary Morstan did little more than hold hands with her future husband, even at the time when their romance was first developing. Possibly the frigidity about which McQueen speculated was brought upon her by a difficult pregnancy and birth. Certainly, domestic scenes are scarce following the marriage. One does not have to stretch the imagination to guess that Mary was relieved to have her husband "innocently" engaged elsewhere and neither pestering her nor pursuing other women. Certainly the post-marital relationship between John and Mary seems, like John Watson's practice, to have been "never very absorbing."[24]

Brend, like most commentators, assumes that Mary was addressing her husband when she referred to "James." He comments only that:

> Wives are…allowed considerable latitude in the names they bestow upon their husbands.[25]

Instead, as noted earlier (see p. 141), we believe she was speaking, not of her husband but of their newly born son.

It is tempting to go on discussing the other major, and some of the minor, commentators on Holmes. Many have noted, without understanding them, the evidences that point to Holmes's femininity and to the complexities of his relationship with Watson, but few provide any data supplementary to our argument. The several attempts at writing partial or complete biographies— and even "autobiographies"—of Holmes[26] and of Watson[27] uniformly fail, since they show no appreciation of the fundamental complexity caused by Holmes's virtually lifelong impersonation.

However, although they may not have succeeded in lifting the veil that Holmes has place over his true features, such authors as Gavin Brend, Martin Dakin, Michael Harrison,[28] James Holroyd,[29] Ian McQueen, Henry C. Potter,[30] Sir Sydney Roberts,[31] and Walter Shepherd[32] have, by their gentle and scholarly probings, added immeasurably to our insight.

The Truth About Sherlock Holmes

IN TEN EARLIER CHAPTERS, we have examined in detail the chronicles of Sherlock Holmes's adventures and have striven to demonstrate her femininity. In an eleventh, we have considered more briefly the writings of major Sherlockian commentators and shown how some of them, at least, were groping toward the truth. Throughout those eleven chapters, we have followed convention by using the masculine forms "he," "him," and "his" in our references to Holmes, even though we are convinced that these pronouns refer only to the role, not to the person. It has been, for us, an awkward convention to adopt, producing absurdities such as references to "his" periods, "his" accouchements, "his" problems with menopause and even "his" pregnancies.

In this final chapter, we shall try concisely to outline the life of Sherlock Holmes, as we believe it truly to have been; and, in doing so, we shall abandon that awkward convention. Instead, we shall consider Sherlock as the woman she was; a woman of great abilities who, in an age when the opportunities for her sex were so limited, needed to act out a lifelong masculine part in order to fulfill her ambitions as a criminal investigator. In doing so, she was to achieve, not merely international renown, but immortality.

It is generally agreed that Sherlock was born in 1854.[1] Friday, 6th January of that year is usually considered to be the date[2] and is accordingly celebrated as "The Birthday" by Sherlockians world-wide. Baring-Gould suggested that

Siger Holmes was the name of her father and that Violet Holmes (nee Sherrinford) was her mother;[3] he believed also that Sherlock had two elder brothers, Sherrinford and Mycroft.[4] However, his identification of Sherlock's parents is questionable at best, and we can find little justification for his belief in that eldest brother. Indeed, so completely did Sherlock succeed in evading any revelations concerning her family that we know only of a relationship with the Vernets, a French family of artists[5] whose English members preferred to style themselves Verner.[6] Even Dr. Watson, though he did come to meet elder brother Mycroft, never learned anything more concerning Sherlock's antecedents—or, if he did learn more, he chose never to expose to us that knowledge.

Nor is there any point, we believe, in searching English parish records for entries under the name "Sherlock Holmes." We may be reasonably sure that Sherlock's surname was Holmes, for was it not shared by brother Mycroft? However, we do *not* believe that "Sherlock" was the name that the Holmes's daughter received at her Christening. Though not an impossible one, it was an unlikely first name to be bestowed in the Victorian era, when there was such stress that proper biblical names should be given to all good Christian children. No; that name was chosen later—and chosen because it was sexually ambiguous, neither definitely feminine nor definitely masculine, yet having a hardness about it, even a harshness, that conveniently suggested masculinity.

"Sherlock" is common enough as a surname in England: the possibilities either that it was a second name, moved into first place (perhaps the surname of her mother?), or that it was adopted because it was a name of a branch of her family cannot be altogether ruled out. However, in those days when relationships were so widely and so seriously studied, such a choice might (in combination with the much more common surname "Holmes") have led an intelligent enquirer to a ready identification of her family. We do not believe that Sherlock would have followed so risky a course.

Instead we believe the name was chosen by the future detective because it was near enough to her true name, yet different enough to serve as concealment.

Maybe it was chosen also because of its symbolism. In the Victorian era, all "proper" women wore their hair long. Short hair was a sign of masculinity: in late Victorian England, the long-haired man was dismissed as effeminate— probably an artist or musician or, even worse, a foreigner! By shearing her locks, Miss Holmes was taking a first, major step toward what was to be a lifelong masquerade. Perhaps her selection of the name was also a first example of that tendency we have noted in earlier chapters—to present a verbal conundrum to the world at large which, if solved, would reveal her secret, whilst remaining secure in the knowledge that it would not be perceived as a conundrum and, consequently, would not be solved.[7]

What was her true name? Well, the nearest feminine appellation, of course, is "Shirley." This was in origin a surname and came only to be adopted as a Christian name after Charlotte Brontë had chosen it for the heiress-heroine of her 1849 novel. Nor did the publication of that novel lead rapidly to any currency for the name in England. As E.G. Withycomb has noted, it first became common as a girl's name in the southern United States, attaining a wider use in North America and the British Isles only because of the popularity of the child film-star, Shirley Temple.[8] Of course, it may have been that Sherlock's mother was—unlike the present writers!—a Brontë fan and somehow persuaded her husband that the name Shirley should be given to her child; yet we do not believe this. Why? Because the names are *too* like; the identification would be *too* readily made.

What, then, would be our choice (for we confess we cannot be certain)? Why, Charlotte! That is a name homophonic to "Sherlock," but sufficiently unlike not to lead at all readily to any identification. Moreover, it was a very respectable name in Victorian times, likely enough to be selected by a family of country squires, such as that from which our heroine sprang. (Had not King George IV's daughter been christened Charlotte?) We suggest that "Charlotte Holmes" is the name for which the English parish records might be searched, for those desirous of establishing the origins of this remarkable lady.

In a spirited survey of the development of girls' fiction, Mary Cadogan and Patricia Craig have so neatly summarized the situation of the mid-Victorian woman that we would like to quote them at length:

> By the middle of the nineteenth century, after the transient licentiousness of its early years, England had settled down firmly to an epoch of respectability. Fashions reflected the emphasis on propriety, and revealing, flimsy dresses had been abandoned in favour of dark silk skirts which expanded as the century progressed. The crinoline almost succeeded in turning women, in actuality, into the kind of female that Queen Victoria represented: a figurehead, stationary and statuesque. Tightly corseted, almost crippled by proliferating underskirts and more covered up than at any time in history, woman expressed in her appearance the image tenaciously projected by male-dominated society of what femininity ought to be.

Despite the challenge and social upheavals of growing industriali-zation, in middle- and upper-class life the cult of the "idle lady" was fashionable.... [To] be idle was the mark of status, and a compliment to the husband or father who "protected" her. Early Victorian men, convinced that they alone were made in the image of God, had become the unchallenged Lords of Creation. Their wives were legally equated with mental defectives and criminals, considered incapable of controlling money, property, children or their own destiny....

In the seclusion of their drawing-rooms, these "genteel" creatures, with no career prospects apart from becoming sadly underpaid governesses or dressmakers, saw marriage as their only fulfillment; therefore they diligently practised those accomplishments intended to endear them to the male. Not surprisingly, female education, whether from untrained governesses at home or at "refined" boarding-schools, consisted mainly of recitation, music, scripture and endless varieties of needlecraft, while the crinoline effectively prevented participation in any sport more vigorous than croquet.[9]

It was into this stultifying environment that Charlotte—for so we will style her, at this earliest stage of her life—was born. Her education left her with some knowledge of classical literature,[10] but otherwise with only one worth-while legacy—a love of music. Elder brother Mycroft was soon sent off to a public school, there to grapple with the Classics (still so all-important to any candidate for high-level appointments); with history and geography (the development of the Empire and the distribution of the British colonies and dependencies that ringed the world); with some respectable modern language (most probably German, in view of the dear Queen's antecedents); and with mathematics. Maybe his education even contained some smidgeon of the other sciences or even, though this is much less likely, included other subjects. And of course, there would have been a good deal of sport; too much, maybe, which might well be the reason for his later sedulous avoidance of exercise!

In contrast, little Charlotte must have been either kept at home, to be taught by a governess or left virtually uninstructed, or else sent to one of those "refined" schools. Whichever happened, she would have received little to challenge or to feed a mind that must, even in early youth, have been exceptionally acute.

As she grew older, there must also have come a time when Charlotte looked into a mirror and performed a ruthless self-evaluation. What she saw cannot have been reassuring. Here was no "sweetly pretty" face, dimpled and delightful, within a cluster of decorative ringlets; here was no fetchingly rounded figure, rendered even more hour-glass-like by tight corsets. Nothing of the kind. Instead, a hawk-like countenance, with square chin and prominent nose, of a sort that no Victorian novelist could ever extol; small breasts, scarcely noticeable; and a long, lean body to which not even the most drastic corseting could give attractive shape. She could not hide it from herself; this was the image of a loser, an also-ran, in the wedlock stakes, destined either for the most unsatisfactory of marriages or for the long tedium of old-maidhood.

It must have been a depressing realization and there may well have been long, secret agonizings and passionate regrets. Yet, at some stage, Charlotte rallied against them and perceived a way out. Yes, indeed she did not look a very feminine woman; why not, then, abandon altogether the attempt to be so? Why not pretend to be a man—seek a man's education, follow a man's career? Why not throw off the shackles that mid-Victorian convention had placed upon her own sex and, instead, seize for herself the freedom, if not the actuality, of masculinity?

When brother Mycroft, now at University, came back with tales of the intellectual opportunities available to male students and of the full and free life of the Colleges, the temptation to Charlotte became too great to resist. So women were debarred from a University education, were they, and only permitted to attend a few lectures of an approved sort? Then it would not be good enough to seek lodgings in Oxford or Cambridge and pick up what few educational crumbs fell from the men's tables. No; she must indeed assume that role she had so long been considering. She must become a man and enroll in a College!

How Charlotte managed it, we do not know. Did Mycroft encourage her or serve as her confidant? It seems highly unlikely; it was not the sort of escapade that any normal mid-Victorian male could possibly approve, if indeed he were capable even of conceiving of it! Though Mycroft was to come to accept Charlotte's role-playing later, and indeed demonstrated some sense of responsibility for her,[11] he was in general to keep aloof. That her parents did not approve is evident, from the completeness with which Charlotte cut adrift from them—or, more probably, was to be cut adrift by them.

All we can say is that, somehow, Charlotte must have found the necessary money—from a legacy, maybe; from some sympathetic female relative or friend; or by the secret and diligent hoarding of chance gifts. Then, we may safely assume, she ran away from home and went off to University.

To which University we cannot be sure, since this also was to remain undisclosed by the chroniclers and has been much argued.[12] However, it was

The rowdy life of London public houses late last century, as here shown in a contemporary print, would not have suited Sherlock.

certainly either Oxford or Cambridge; no other alternative is possible. Admission requirements were light in those days, at least in the less fashionable colleges; there were no exams to be passed, no requirements for a satisfactory record of school performances. Provided that Charlotte—or "Sherlock," as she had now become—was able convincingly to demonstrate that she had some sort of an aristocratic or land-owning background and managed somehow to cope with the inevitable questions about sporting achievements, she would be admitted.

After admission, however, she would have found herself in an alarmingly unfamiliar environment. It would have been easy enough for her to attend lectures—or, indeed, *not* to attend them, whenever her physical condition made attendance difficult. Many male students of that time, and of later times also, rarely troubled to do so. Moreover, with her acute brain, Sherlock would have

The mild, aristocratic Reginald Musgrave—and uncommonly handsome!
(The Musgrave Ritual)

been able to excel in the tutorials (though the tutors would be somewhat puzzled by her lack of any classical training).

But the social life of the College; ah! that was something else! Admittedly, participation in sports and in heavy drinking sessions might be avoided; there was no need to become a "hearty." However, if one did not join those drinking parties, and especially if one were identified as unnaturally reclusive, one was likely to be marked down to be the butt of the heavy-handed jokes and the "japes" perpetrated by those sporty and sportive young gentlemen.

We suspect that one such incident—a de-bagging, perhaps—led to a startled recognition of Sherlock's femininity, an embarrassing and embarrassed interview with the Warden of the College or his deputy, and a surreptitious, swift dismissal from College and University. No wonder Sherlock was so careful to conceal the name of her University; the memory of her humiliation would ensure such a response!

Before this disaster happened, however, there had developed a casual acquaintance with the mild, aristocratic Reginald Musgrave and that more rewarding, bulldog-generated friendship with the very masculine, if somewhat shy, Victor Trevor. The latter, in particular, was to play a crucial part in Holmes's life; for it was during that month spent at the Trevors' home in Norfolk that Sherlock's acute powers of observation first manifested themselves, leading to her recognition of the possibility of a career in the detection of crime.

In the meantime, there was the humiliation of defeat to be endured. Sherlock could not bear to return to her parents. Quite likely, had she done so in a sufficiently abject state of contrition, she would have been readmitted to the household; but to face what a life! No, that was not to be contemplated; and, after all, there was still a little money in hand. So Sherlock reluctantly became Charlotte again and, resuming feminine attire, took those rooms in Montague Street. For self-protection against gossip or worse, she assumed temporarily another role, that of the married woman "Mrs. Holmes."

Quite soon, however, her confidence returned. She reassumed both masculine attire and the appellation Sherlock; she found new lodgings—though not very satisfactory ones; and she began a campaign of intensive reading and practical work in science. Her studies may have seemed desultory and eccentric to others (young Stamford, for example[13]) but they had a definite object—to give her a firm basis of knowledge in all subjects that might be necessary in the investigation of crime and the identification of criminals.

The work proceeded well—so well, indeed, that she was permitted to begin those original researches that led to the recognition of the reagent precipitated only by haemoglobin.[14] However, the digs were unsatisfactory and money was dwindling. After much searching, Sherlock found ideal alternative quarters—with a kindly and competent, but satisfactorily unimaginative, landlady called Mrs. Hudson, on the upper floors of no. 221 Baker Street.

The problem was the cost; this was outside her present financial reach. It would be necessary for her to find someone to go halves with. In an age where respectability was so overwhelmingly important, that someone could not, in view of the role Sherlock was adopting, be a woman. No, it must be a man; someone solidly respectable, with an income steady enough to enable him reliably to pay his way and without the sort of imaginative percipience that would enable him to penetrate Sherlock's disguise. Someone, indeed, just like Dr. John H. Watson!

Thus, essentially for financial reasons and through the chance intercession of young Stamford, did an acquaintance begin that was to ripen eventually into something much more.

At the beginning of their occupation of 221B, Sherlock took extreme precautions to keep her life and Watson's as separate as was possible in shared quarters. She was careful that Watson should move in first, so that there was no danger of their luggage being confused and the wrong suitcase being unpacked; she rose each morning significantly earlier or significantly later than Watson, to ensure no unguarded and embarrassing bathroom encounters; and, in general, she kept out of Watson's way as much as possible during the day—at the chemical laboratory, in the dissecting rooms, or on those investigative visits to "the lowest portions of the city," which the innocent Watson thought merely to be long, oddly directed walks.[15]

Such walks were hazardous enough during the daylight, even for a man: indeed, Sherlock's taking of them was in itself an adventure, a defiance, as well as an exploration of the breeding grounds of crime. At night, they would be impossibly dangerous—and the laboratories were closed. She could not risk applying for membership of a club, of the sort to which the males of her class so regularly resorted; no, not even the Diogenes Club, much though it might have suited her tastes, for brother Mycroft was a member already and would not have permitted it. Moreover, she was too fastidious to wish to spend her evenings in a public house, among drunks and in an atmosphere thick with tobacco smoke. So it was necessary to return to 221B and trust that Watson might be out. If he were not, Sherlock went early to bed, so as to reduce the times of leisure with Watson during which she might have suffered embarrassing inquisitions. Moreover, rather because the habit of secrecy was growing on her than for any better reason, she concealed from Watson the true character of her daily occupations.

Naturally enough, however, the under-engaged Watson became increasingly curious about Sherlock. Even though not perceiving the true significance of those recurrent phases of "idleness" during which Sherlock, whose menstrual cycle was always to give her serious problems, had to spend days on end lying silent on the sofa—a strange failure, for a medical man!—Watson did note other oddities.

When taxed by a surprised Watson on matters regarding which her minimal education had told her nothing—the Copernican Theory and the composition of the Solar System, for example[16]—Sherlock excused herself by pretending that, yes, she had known this—must have known it—but had deliberately forgotten because such topics were irrelevant to her work. Moreover, she continued to exhibit sufficient testiness to discourage any further probings.

It was only after several weeks that Sherlock revealed to Watson the nature of her profession. This happened because of Watson's inadvertent tactlessness. Sherlock had attempted to put onto paper an outline of the methods of observation she was developing and, having written the article, had submitted it hesitantly as an anonymous contribution to one of London's many magazines. She was delighted when it was published and, in typically feminine fashion, left the magazine where Watson would see it.

The ambitious title of the article, *The Book of Life*, did indeed catch his eye. However, he reacted not with the praise Sherlock had hoped for, but with contempt, calling it "ineffable twaddle!"[17]

Well, Watson could not be allowed to get away with that! So Sherlock displayed to him her powers of observation and deduction, in a manner that he found not only convincing but also entirely fascinating. When Watson mentioned his own particular fictional idols, Edgar Allan Poe's Dupin and Gaboriau's Lecoq, Sherlock avenged herself for that earlier slight by dismissing the one as "a very inferior fellow" and the other as "a miserable bungler." Then, perceiving with malicious satisfaction Watson's indignation, she proceeded to a further and even more devastatingly convincing display of her own powers by correctly identifying the retired sergeant of Marines.[18]

At this, Watson's stupefaction was gratifyingly marked and his praise unstinted. This was so delightful to her—after all, poor Sherlock had been starved of admiration for so much of her difficult life—that, following a brief and very feminine pretence at reluctance, Sherlock elected to respond to the summons brought by the ex-sergeant. Not only that, but she took Watson with her. The summons was to investigate the murder of the unattractive American, Enoch J. Drebber. When Watson was so much impressed that he even decided to write an account of the case, Sherlock's victory was complete.[19]

Sherlock had no least intention of revealing her true sex to Watson, for to do so would be to risk being patronized or even laughed at by him. Yet—yes, it *would* be nice to have an admirer to hand, to utter words of congratulation whenever they were merited and to pay her the more enduring tribute of chronicling her successes.

However, Sherlock's decision was not made swiftly: the habit of secrecy remained too strong for it to be easy for her to accept a companion in her adventures. Over the next six years, Watson, found only four cases to chronicle and was only once invited on a journey away from London.[20] There may, of course, have been other joint adventures, but if so they must surely have been few and not particularly interesting.

We believe there was another reason also for this reluctance to involve Watson; that Sherlock had fallen in love, as passionately as was possible for her, with some other male. Was it Victor Trevor, perhaps—that man who was her "very opposite...in most respects"?[21]—after all, it is well known that opposites attract! Or was it the gentle, aristocratic Reginald Musgrave, a type of man likely enough to be fascinated by an intelligent, strong-minded woman and handsome enough to attract her? Whoever it was, Sherlock gave herself to him all too freely, in some moment when her defenses were down; such impulsive givings are not unusual even today, in women of what was then called the "bluestocking" type. Unfortunately for poor Sherlock, as has so often happened at that era and others, she did so only to find herself pregnant and discarded.

There followed that hasty trip to France, where facilities might be found for procuring a miscarriage or, after a discreet accouchement, for arranging an equally discreet "adoption" of the child. During the slow, solitary recovery in that hotel room in Lyons,[22] Sherlock found herself understandably in a state of physical reaction and mental depression. Into her mind came the thought of the faithful Watson, honest and eager to help; so he was summoned to her aid. By hastening across to France, Watson demonstrated his devotion and endeared himself deeply to her.

Yet Watson could not be altogether trusted, so soon after a betrayal by another of his sex; no, her secret must still be concealed from him! However, from then onward, Watson was regularly to be accepted, even sought, as a companion in her adventures. This was not, we may be sure, merely because he served as whetstone to Sherlock's sharper mind, but because she found his solid, reliable—and male—company reassuring.

The change is marked indeed. In the previous six years (1881–1887), Watson had found only four investigations worthy of record, even if he had been involved in others. In the ensuing four years (1887–1891), he was to chronicle no fewer than twenty-one! Yes, Sherlock's practice was gaining impetus and, within certain specialized circles, her name becoming renowned; but that cannot have been the reason for so marked a disparity. No; the truth is that, after the return from France, Sherlock—even if she might at times find his slowness of perception tiresome—was urgently desiring John Watson's companionship. We may be sure, indeed, that she wanted much more from him; but alas! she felt still too vulnerable to admit him into her secret and her bed.

Even when that night in Birlstone[23] provided the opportunity of a shared room, Sherlock hesitated and, hesitating, lost. Off she went on that solitary walk. When she came back and approached Watson's bed, she balked, launched forth into that curious rigmarole of words (see p. 25), and slunk away in lonely silence.

Then came catastrophe. Watson, after seven dilatory years, had at last written and published the account of his first adventure with Sherlock—the adventure which he christened *A Study in Scarlet*. It appeared at a time when Sherlock's career had reached such a point of stagnation that she had started dosing herself intravenously with drugs, sometimes morphine, sometimes cocaine; these were not illegal in Britain at that time. Unfortunately for both of them, on that fateful September afternoon in 1888, Watson chose to rebuke Sherlock for her drug habit before raising the topic of his book.

Whether through resentment of his criticism or whether because, in Sherlock's retentive memory, there was still burning a spark of resentment of Watson's forthright criticism of her own first published opus, she did not praise Watson's tribute to her abilities. Instead, she poured upon his first-born work the icy water of her criticism:

> "I glanced over it.... Honestly, I cannot congratulate you upon it. Detection is, or ought to be, an exact science and should be treated in the same cold and unemotional manner. You have attempted to tinge it with romanticism, which produces much the same effect as if you worked a love-story or an elopement into the fifth proposition of Euclid."
>
> "But the romance was there," I remonstrated. "I could not tamper with the facts."
>
> "Some facts should be suppressed, or, at least, a just sense of proportion should be observed in treating them. The only point in the case which deserved mention was the curious analytical reasoning from effects to causes, by which I succeeded in unravelling it."[24]

One cannot wonder that Watson was deeply hurt by the reception of this, his greatest tribute to his friend; who would not be? One cannot wonder, either, that he was irritated by this demonstration of Sherlock's egotism, then at its most extreme.

Moreover, Sherlock proceeded to pour salt into Watson's gaping emotional wound by first showing to him a letter of fulsome praise from the French detective, François de Villard, and then trivializing Watson's own attainment by mentioning the "several monographs" which she had published, but which she had not troubled even to show to Watson.[25] Finally, she took pains to demonstrate again to him her mental superiority, by the feat of reasoning concerning his visit to Wigmore Street.[26] All of which may have reduced Watson to a state of what she might have considered proper humility; but certainly, it would not heal that deep wound to his self-esteem. Quite the contrary.

Maybe this behaviour can, in a fashion, be excused; maybe it stemmed, in part from Sherlock's long enduring, in close proximity, of desires that she still did not dare admit to Watson. Yet the result was predictable. When spurned by one woman, a man swiftly finds for himself another; very many marriages are made, in Heaven possibly, but certainly on the rebound. Watson was not aware that Sherlock was a woman, yet their relationship had been settling into something very close to a marriage. He had intended a tribute; it had been insultingly rejected. Naturally enough, Watson was left feeling betrayed.

And, of course, though neither of them knew it, Watson and Sherlock were on the threshold of being drawn into the affair of *The Sign of the Four*, in which Watson was to meet the attractive Miss Mary Morstan—a damsel in distress, available to be defended by the doughty and romantic Watson (albeit with Sherlock's aid) and so entirely and refreshingly different from his long-time room-mate! Well, the consequence was inevitable. Before the case ended, Watson was engaged to be married and Sherlock had lost all she had gained from him—never enough, of course, but a great deal.

Predictably, Watson received no congratulations from Sherlock on his engagement, even if she did pay a grudging tribute to Miss Morstan's charms. Instead, Sherlock retreated into her intellectual ivory tower—carrying with her the syringe and the supply of drugs.

The single adventure that intervened between the announcement of the engagement and the marriage showed Sherlock in more philosophic mood. She had endured enough, in childhood and youth, to have become by temperament a survivor—but she knew well that, without Watson's company, the future would be bleak for her.

Did Sherlock attend the nuptial ceremonies of John and Mary? It seems unlikely; no doubt some urgent investigation was embarked upon, or invented, to enable Sherlock to avoid them. Did she send a wedding gift? Probably; to omit to do so would have been an inadmissible slight upon one with whom she must have hoped, at least, to remain on friendly terms. (We wonder what that gift may have been—something conventional and expensive, no doubt, but what?) Certainly, for many months after the wedding, she avoided the newlywed couple; and Watson, wrapped as he was in that new, warm blanket of connubial bliss, was scarcely even aware of the fact.

When Watson did return, more or less by chance, to 221B, Sherlock's reactions were initially ambiguous;[27] she seems scarcely to have known whether she was glad or sorry to see him. Yet his coming was a reminder of earlier, happier times and it was a renewed pleasure to have him alongside her in an investigation. So much so, indeed, that she realized she could not excise him from her life. She needed him, even if he did not need—or was not aware that he needed—her.

Within a few months, there came the opportunity of the crime in Boscombe Valley; could Watson be inveigled away from his wife for a few days? So he was sent that telegram of invitation. For all her other abilities, Sherlock did not really know how to write it, and Watson may well have been puzzled by its curious phraseology. Nonetheless Mary Watson, still grateful to Sherlock and quite unsuspecting, actually urged her husband to go![28]

Watson may have gone off to Devonshire with Sherlock, but he was still deeply in love with Mary. After a gap of many years he resumed his medical career, buying a decayed practice in Paddington and devoting himself so sedulously to it that, for a while at least, it was a success. Then along came baby James to make the marital relationship more binding.

Yet things were soon beginning to go wrong between them. Little James died in early infancy; and, though most Victorian couples managed to endure such losses and replace the lost child with an amplitude of successors, John and Mary had no other children. Perhaps Mary felt a particular bitterness; since her husband was a doctor, surely he above all men should have been able to save their son's life? It is possible that, in reaction, Mary lapsed into frigidity; or maybe, though they sought for a while to have a second child, they quite simply failed. Whatever the cause, a strain developed between John and Mary.

This was, of course, Sherlock's opportunity. She began to visit the Watson household, when Mary was there or—with greater enthusiasm, no doubt!—at times when Mary was absent or had retired to bed. When in September 1899 Mary went away to visit an aunt, John was cordially invited to stay with Sherlock at 221B.[29] Afterwards he returned to his home in Kensington for a while—but only for a matter of months. By the following April he was back in Baker Street, not as a guest but in residence.[30]

Sherlock is threatened with destruction—but not with death—by Professor James Moriarty. (The Final Problem)

Yet the breach between Mary and he proved temporary. Holmes's intellectual charms were not sufficient altogether to compensate for the loss of Mary's physical ones and Watson, moreover, had a strong sense of duty. Back he went to Kensington. Next time it needed Sherlock's pretence that she was dying to bring Watson back to 221B;[31] nor did he stay.

Sherlock was, we may presume, deeply upset when, having twice lured back the man she loved—once briefly and a second time for a long stay—she could not keep him. Now it was her turn for a rebound.

Who was it that she met? Did she encounter Victor Trevor again, or the aristocratic Reginald? Was it someone who has passed quite unmentioned in the Chronicles? Or did she, as we have suggested earlier, succumb for a while—willingly or reluctantly—to the ruthless masculine force of Colonel Sebastian Moran?

The latter is the alternative that we favour, for we believe that the scene in which Sherlock first encountered that "Napoleon of crime," Professor James Moriarty, has a significance hitherto unperceived. Sherlock described it thus:

> "My nerves are fairly proof, Watson, but I must confess to a start when I saw the very man who had been so much in my thoughts standing there on my threshold…. He peered at me with great curiosity in his puckered eyes.
>
> "You have less frontal development than I should have expected," said he at last. "It is a dangerous habit to finger loaded fire-arms in the pocket of one's dressing-gown."[32]

It has been assumed hitherto that Moriarty was looking at Sherlock's head when he made that remark; but we believe his eyes were aimed in a quite different direction. We believe that he knew well that Sherlock had been either seduced or raped by Moran and was now bearing the Colonel's child. If Moriarty had been gazing at Sherlock's head, why was it that he was perceiving the revolver *in the pocket of her dressing-gown?*

No, his eyes were looking much lower. He was seeking for visible evidences that Sherlock was "in a certain condition," as the Victorians so carefully phrased it—and he was not finding them. Some women, of course, give surprisingly little external indication of pregnancy, even when it is several months advanced; and Sherlock was evidently one of them.

Let us consider also the conversation that followed. Professor Moriarty had already been, by his own admission, seriously incommoded by Sherlock's manoeuvres and was well aware that Sherlock had amassed enough evidence to destroy his criminal organization. However, he was equally aware of Holmes's condition and its cause. He did not threaten Sherlock with death; instead, he threatened to "destroy" her—to destroy her public image and her practice, so carefully built up over so many years, by arranging some public revelation of her femininity and of her pregnancy. However, the Professor was still willing to bargain; to hold his hand, if Sherlock would cease her pursuit of him and his minions:

> "You must drop it, Mr. Holmes," said he, swaying his face about. "You really must, you know."

"After Monday," said I.

"Tut, tut!" said he "I am quite sure that a man of your intelligence will see that there can be but one outcome to this affair. It is necessary that you withdraw. You have worked things in such a fashion that we have only one resource left. It has been an intellectual treat for me to see the way in which you have grappled with this affair, and I say, unaffectedly, that it would be grief to me to be forced to undertake any extreme measure. You smile, sir, but I assure you that it really would."

"Danger is part of my trade," I remarked.

"That is not danger," said he. "It is inevitable destruction. You stand in the way not merely of an individual, but of a mighty organization, the full extent of which you, with all your cleverness, have been unable to realize.... If you are clever enough to bring destruction upon me, rest assured that I shall do as much for you."[33]

We may almost hear the irony in his voice when he stressed "*Mr.* Holmes"; "a *man* of your intelligence," and so forth. Notice, however, that Moriarty did not expect to die himself and was not threatening Sherlock with death. Moriarty was fearing the destruction of all he had achieved and, in retaliation, was threatening Sherlock with the destruction of all she had achieved.

What laughter there would be, what jibes and sneers, if the truth came out! Though she was determined to destroy Moriarty and root out the evil he had wrought, Sherlock could not risk that. So it was that she had conceived already the play to be enacted somewhere on the European continent. Her plans had been formulated most carefully, yet they were to come close to going awry.

There was a further complication for Sherlock in that—whatever had occurred to terminate her first pregnancy—we believe that, this time, she had decided to bear her child and to rear it. That would be a compensation for the loss of her practice, should the truth about her be revealed; she could remain in France and engage in an entirely novel occupation.

If this was the case, it might seem to be an argument against Colonel Moran being the father; would Sherlock truly wish to rear the Colonel's child? Since, though noting the Colonel's fine pedigree and "honourable career" in the Indian Army, Sherlock was to suggest that his sudden turn to evil reflected his heredity,[34] such a decision might not appear very likely. Yet that judgement was pronounced three years later; it was a judgement in hindsight, after intervening years of bitterness and betrayal. Moreover, in 1891 Sherlock was thirty-seven years old; she must have known it was unlikely she would have another child, if this one were to be aborted. We believe she decided to chance its heredity and to bear Moran's child, however it had come to be conceived.

In her planning of her journey, Sherlock was aided by the worsening relations between John and Mary Watson. Yes, John had returned to Kensington. However, with his declining enthusiasm for his marriage, he was putting much less effort into his practice. The surgery in Paddington had to be closed, for it was not bringing in money enough to pay the rent, and the Kensington house had to be sold. Instead, Watson began practising from a consulting-room in his new home in Mortimer Street.[35] This decline in style of living did nothing to strengthen the already seriously ailing marriage. After a few months, Mary found the situation intolerable and left him.

Yes, Watson told Sherlock that his wife was gone "on a visit,"[36] and maybe that was a half-truth. However, it was no normal visit. Why, when Sherlock invited him to go along for that week on the Continent, Watson neither troubled to inform his wife of what he was doing nor even wrote to her from Europe! No; we may be sure that Mary had left in a huff, vowing never to return. Maybe that vow was not to be taken seriously—such vows rarely are—but it left John sufficiently angry to make his own act of defiance by slipping away with Sherlock.

Of course, Sherlock had known the condition of their marriage and had been aware of Mary's departure. Consequently, Sherlock had been able to calculate how John Watson would react—and had calculated rightly.

She had deduced also that Moriarty would expect her to stay in London till the following Monday, in order that she might witness her triumph. Consequently, having visited Sherlock on the Friday, Moriarty would be arranging for her public humiliation to take place on the Saturday or the Sunday. It became necessary, therefore, for Holmes to flee England at once—and to do so, if possible, without Moriarty being aware of it.

When Sherlock visited Watson on that fateful Friday evening, she had two reasons to take care not to be seen. First, as she proclaimed, she desired to avoid Moriarty's spies. Second, however, she wished to make sure that, if the truth about her were indeed to be revealed, the innocent Watson would not be suspected of having fathered her child.

Yet a new trouble came upon her. Perhaps simply because of the emotional strains Sherlock had been undergoing but also, maybe, because of a physical strain suffered when she left the Watson home and clambered over that back wall into Mortimer Street,[37] Sherlock found herself developing symptoms suggesting an imminent miscarriage. That was why Mycroft Holmes, seriously concerned about his sister's condition, roused himself from his customary indolence. Not only did he attire himself as a coachman in order to take his disguised sister safely to her train, but he even went back to fetch Watson, so that Sherlock would not have to travel to the Continent unescorted.

Watson, we may note in passing, failed as usual to penetrate Sherlock's disguise and was, as usual, astonished when she revealed herself.[38] It was a scene destined to be repeated several more times.

However, Sherlock had by no means recovered. After mischievously enjoying her game with Watson, she began again to feel those threatening internal cramps. She had anticipated Moriarty's pursuit and had planned, on leaving the train at Canterbury, to travel cross-country to Newhaven;[39] but there was need for her to rest. Having left their train at Canterbury and witnessed the passing of Moriarty's special—no, she had not managed to leave London unobserved— she and Watson were delayed through the whole afternoon by Sherlock's need for food, rest and recuperation. Only after several hours was she fit to enter a conveyance and to travel the bumpy roads to Newhaven. In consequence, it was night before they reached Brussels,[40] by a later boat and train than had been planned. Moreover, they spent two days in the Belgian capital and, when travelling onward, went only as far as Strasbourg on the first day.[41]

These rests served their purpose; the threat of a miscarriage was averted. However, in other respects all was not going well. Holmes had telegraphed to the London police on the Monday morning, to enquire how far they had succeeded in rounding up the Moriarty gang. When she received a telegram in reply:

> Holmes tore it open, and then with a bitter curse tossed it into the grate.
> "I might have known it," [s]he groaned. "He has escaped!"
> "Moriarty!"
> "They have secured the whole gang, with the exception of him. He has given them the slip. Of course, when I left the country there was no one to cope with him. But I did think that I had put the game in their hands. I think you had better return to London, Watson."
> "Why?"
> "Because you will find me a dangerous companion now...."[42]

This exchange makes it clear that Sherlock had considered it quite vital that she leave London, even though knowing that no-one but herself could properly scotch Moriarty. In other words, the necessity for escaping the threat of exposure overrode the urgency of ensuring that the master criminal was arrested. Sherlock had first to guard her own reputation and so must—while having not much faith that they would do it properly—entrust the London police with the task of completing her work. Moreover, only *after* the net had closed and Moriarty had escaped it did Sherlock feel in danger of her life—and that, despite the pursuing special train. Only from that time did she become a dangerous companion for Watson—never before.

We may perceive also that, for her own reasons, Sherlock was not telling Watson the whole truth. As she knew well, one other major figure in the Moriarty gang had escaped the police net; but then, he was someone whose capture she had never intended!

So, since Watson insisted (to Sherlock's deep gratification) in remaining with her and sharing the risk, they travelled onward that night to Geneva in Switzerland. They spent what Watson called "a charming week" in the Rhône Valley, travelled over the snow-covered Gemmi Pass and, after visiting Interlaken, reached Meiringen, where that final scene was to be enacted.[43] It was while they were crossing the Gemmi that some stones fell, by natural chance or by human design. This caused Sherlock to reflect aloud to her friend on the career which, she believed, was ending:

> "I think that I may go as far as to say, Watson, that I have not lived
> wholly in vain.... If my record were closed to-night I could still survey
> it with equanimity. The air of London is the sweeter for my presence.
> In over a thousand cases I am not aware that I have ever used my
> powers on the wrong side. Of late I have been tempted to look into the
> problems furnished by Nature rather than these more superficial ones
> for which our artificial state of society is responsible...."[44]

Indeed so; was she not on the threshold of abandoning her career as a detective, and even her pretence of being a male, in order to face the very different challenges of being a mother and rearing a child with a recognizedly difficult heredity?

Yet, before Sherlock embarked upon this new task, she had to deal finally with Moriarty. At the same time, moreover, she needed to sever her relations with Watson in a fashion that would leave him convinced that she, his friend, was dead. The final scene that she had planned, on the assumption that Moriarty would have been entrapped in London, may well have simply involved an accident in some wild place. Now, with the Professor to be dealt with as well, there was need to improvise—and Sherlock managed this brilliantly.

Sherlock by the Reichenbach Falls, awaiting those encounters with two enemies—or an enemy and a lover? (The Final Problem)

Her account of the closing scene, and Watson's, may both be trusted up to a point, we feel. Yes, Watson and Sherlock *did* walk along the flanks of the Rhine, there confined into a torrent, to witness its spectacular plunge down the Reichenbach Falls. Yes, Watson *was* summoned back to his hotel by a bogus note, leaving Sherlock to face Moriarty alone. And yes, there *was* a struggle which resulted in Moriarty plunging into the falls, leaving Sherlock gasping but unhurt on their rim.[45]

(Incidentally, if Sherlock had been as skilled in combat as she claimed, why was it so desperate a struggle? Why, when Moriarty rushed at her in a fashion suggesting no ability in fighting but only frantic animosity, did she not use her skills in boxing or in baritsu, that strangely-styled Japanese wrestling system, to fell the evil Professor before he closed with her? Once again, we have reason to question those vaunted skills of Sherlock's!)

After that, though, we take leave to question the veracity of her subsequent account to Watson. We believe that she had made her arrangements already with Colonel Moran, the formidable but unscrupulous person who had fathered her child. When did she do this? While there is no direct indication, we believe that it may well have been on the afternoon of the Friday, following that encounter with Moriarty; there are several hours unaccounted for between the sinister Professor's departure and Sherlock's arrival in Watson's consulting-room. If she were not so engaged, what else was she doing during those hours? Why did she delay seeking Watson and fleeing with him to the Continent? Sherlock was not the sort of woman to take overmuch time over her packing and the arrangements with Mycroft, if not already made, would not have taken long. (Indeed, we believe that Sherlock did not seek out her brother until late in the evening, after that scramble over the wall, when her physical distress was mounting.)

Very well, then; what is our evidence that there *was* an arrangement with Colonel Moran? We have mentioned already (p. 55) Sherlock's words to Watson— that only one man, Moriarty, had escaped the police net; but there are further indications that support our thesis.

After the (literal) downfall of Moriarty, Sherlock climbed perilously to a ledge some way above the path, so that her returning tracks would not be seen. As she lay recovering from her exertion—of course, her condition was such that she would tire easily, and recent events had been truly stressful—the Colonel tried to kill her by rolling stones down upon her.[46] Or so Sherlock was later to claim!

Yet her story does not bear scrutiny. Was it logical that Colonel Sebastian Moran, that magnificent shot, that renowned *shikari*, would have chosen such an uncertain method, when a well-placed bullet would not only have avenged his chief so much more effectively but also ensured his own security? Both on the path and on the ledge, Sherlock would have been in full view. Her body, if it did not immediately tumble into the Falls, could have been tossed there readily enough. After passing through the Falls, it would be so battered that no mark of a shot would be noticed. With the cause of death so obvious, why should there have been any post-mortem?

No, that story won't do. Probably it was suggested by the earlier incident in the Gemmi Pass, when either mere chance or some maladroit member of the Moriarty gang had caused the fall of stones. We believe instead that at the Reichenbach Falls, the Colonel either threw down some stones to attract Sherlock's attention or dislodged them inadvertently when clambering down to join her on the ledge.

Perhaps he climbed down to aid her; more probably, however, it was to confirm their arrangement—to make sure that he was not now under any threat from the London police. We believe that Sherlock, despite her awareness of the crimes the Colonel had committed and despite what she had suffered from him, had nevertheless afforded him the chance to correct that twist from the irreproachable path of his earlier life and go straight. We believe that, in return for his promise to do so, Sherlock had suppressed the evidence against him—not from altruism, but because he was her child's father.

After this meeting, what happened? Well, certainly Sherlock and the Colonel parted, he to return to London in clear knowledge that he was not in danger of arrest, she to seek refuge—not from the Moriarty gang, but from prying eyes and wagging tongues—in France and, immediately or ultimately in Montpellier. There, we believe, her child was born, probably after a difficult and exhausting labour; there the infant lived out its short life; and there, after a few poignant years, it died, leaving Sherlock free again, but desolated.

At about that time, Sherlock read in the newspapers[47] of the slaying of Ronald Adair at the Bagatelle Club in London—and she noted, among the names of those who had been playing cards with him, that of Colonel Sebastian Moran. So the Colonel had not kept his promise! And their child—the child in whom he had shown no least interest—had died. There was doubly reason why Sherlock should seek revenge, for had she not been twice betrayed?

So she planned her return to England and made sure, by a method never revealed to Watson, that the Colonel would be aware of her plan. Sherlock did not need to warn Moran that she would be able to find evidence that would convict him, either of this crime or of earlier crimes; he knew that well enough.

His only recourse was to try to murder Sherlock before she could expose him. And so Colonel Moran was lured, like the tigers he had once hunted, to a baited trap—and caught.

We may note that after his capture, when Sherlock was addressing those teasing words to her former lover (see p. 82), she mentioned, not his having tried to kill her above the Reichenbach Falls, but merely that he had favoured her with his attentions there![48] The phrasing not only supports our thesis, but also leaves room for speculation as to what exactly did happen on that ledge.

And so the Colonel was led away by the police, out of Sherlock's life. Yet, curiously, he was not hanged for his crime, as would have been usual; did Sherlock intercede for him, even then? Instead, Moran was merely sent for a prolonged sojourn in prison. He was still alive, though probably still within prison walls, in 1914 when he gained his last mention in the chronicles.[49] However, he troubled Sherlock no more.

The prime motivation for Sherlock's return to London, then, was a desire for revenge; but there was a second, happier reason. Brother Mycroft had been watching over his sister's affairs and making sure that the lodgings at 221B Baker Street were kept in readiness for her return.[50] (Even the kindly but slow-witted Mrs. Hudson must sometimes have wondered—convinced as she was that Sherlock was dead—why she was being paid rent and required to keep the rooms unaltered and clean!) From Mycroft, Sherlock had learned some news that should have been saddening but was instead quite exhilarating—that Mary Watson had died. John Watson was free again; the partnership could be resumed and, with good fortune, might become much more!

And yes, John Watson was delighted—even, initially, overwhelmed[51]—by Sherlock's return. He had patched up the quarrel with Mary, but the last years of their marriage had been difficult, at best. With Sherlock back and their rooms at 221B as it had always been—why, it was like a welcome step backward into happier years! Soon he was again in residence in Baker Street with Sherlock.

For something less than three years, John Watson maintained some semblance of independence by continuing his medical practice, now again located in Kensington. However, Sherlock required a full-time partner and John was happy to accommodate himself to that role. Eventually he sold his practice, and for a good price. It was only later that he was to learn that the purchaser, a young doctor named Verner, was not merely a relative of Sherlock's but had even been using her money for the puchase.[52]

At about that time, Sherlock lowered the last barriers between John and herself, revealing to him her femininity. With this revelation and what followed from it, their relationship naturally mellowed. Sherlock was happier than she had ever been, capable of joking and even exhibiting what, in her, passed for tenderness and affection. Both of them had gone through difficult times; this was an episode of tranquillity.

Yet John was a normal man, with a normal man's appetites, while Sherlock was essentially a rather passionless, cerebral creature. Moreover, with the approach of menopause, Sherlock became again difficult to live with, increasingly moody—at best her normal, cool self, at worst impatient, demanding, bitter-tongued and thoroughly unreasonable.

It was typical of her jealous moodiness that, when suspecting Watson of even a passing interest in another woman, Sherlock found an excuse for sending him abroad; then, worrying about the liaisons he might be forming there, pursued him; and, having found him and found her suspicions unjustified, proceeded immediately to upbraid him for his inadequacies![53]

Nevertheless, the loyal and patient Watson endured Sherlock's moods and gibes surprisingly long. He was even at times capable of playing the dominant role in their partnership, as when Sherlock strove to exclude him from participation in the burgling of the blackmailer Milverton's house and was overridden, to her own secret pleasure.[54] While they were waiting in the darkness of Milverton's study, she was even to seek the physical reassurance of Watson's touch—for that was what happened, even if Watson reported it otherwise.

Moreover, there still remained times when Sherlock displayed her affection for Watson. In their Dartmoor encounter after many days of separation, when Watson became justifiably angry with her, Sherlock did not respond with reciprocal anger; instead, she took pains to wheedle him back into a better mood.[55] And when Watson was shot, she showed her concern for him in a fashion that touched him deeply—making it clear also that, if he had died or had been seriously injured, he would have been swiftly avenged.[56]

Yet ultimately the stresses of their relationship became unendurable for Watson. Sometime between July and September of 1902, he walked out on Sherlock and took lodgings in Queen Anne Street.[57] He was never again to be lured back into residence at 221B. Though he did continue to play a part in Sherlock's cases from time to time, it was with diminishing frequency and enthusiasm.

Moreover, we have it on Sherlock's own authority that, by January of 1903, Watson had found for himself a wife. Though Sherlock makes it explicit that she felt herself deserted,[58] she was otherwise much less specific. Had Watson embarked upon a second marriage, or was he having an affair with another man's wife? We are inclined to believe the latter and we suspect his *inamorata* may have been Mrs. Neville St. Clair, to whom Watson had so unaffectedly shown himself attracted thirteen years earlier.[59] Her husband may well have died in the meantime, but he was evidently a difficult person and she might simply have left him, thus inspiring Watson's sympathy without troubling his honest conscience.

Whoever the lady was, it is likely that Watson's developing relationship with her was the eventual cause for his move to Queen Anne Street—maybe, indeed, into her house. It would be interesting to know the names of any ladies, married or unmarried, who owned property in that street during that year!

By this time, Sherlock knew herself to be undergoing menopause: as we have noted, its onset may well have been the unrealized cause for her earlier moodiness and irritability. The departure of Watson was a bitter blow, in part because she was herself now inclined to a sensuality earlier unknown, in part because in other respects her powers, physical and mental, were declining. Sherlock needed a man in her life to carry her through this difficult phase—and she had lost the one she desired.

Yes, Watson was persuaded into participation in a few more adventures, but he was reluctant and Sherlock's performances were not impressive. Watson did write up the affair of *The Red Circle*, but as an investigation it was pretty much of a shambles[60] and he found little in it to interest him. Thereafter he witnessed, without properly comprehending, Sherlock's defeat by Isadora Klein in the affair of *The Three Gables*.[61] (That was also the adventure during which Watson manifested such extreme distaste for Holmes's friend, the man who styled himself 'Langdale Pike').[62] These were not cases likely to renew in Watson the old sense of excitement, of privilege at being a participant in Sherlock's investigations; quite the contrary.

As for Sherlock, she was seeking desperately for a new partner, someone to replace Watson. We may suspect, without being sure, that her "illness" at the time of *The Mazarin Stone*[63] may have been a natural miscarriage following a belated romantic episode. This was quite possibly (though by no means certainly) with Watson; but if so, the episode was all too brief. The page Billy of that adventure may well have served for her a substitute for the child she had lost twelve years earlier; he would have been about the right age. After a while, however, Billy seems to have found the role too oppressive and left for an easier position, for he is not again mentioned.

The last joint adventure with Watson for more than a decade was, symbolically enough, the affair of *The Creeping Man*; of the Professor who sought, for reasons of sexual desire, to make himself young again—and could not manage it. Watson, summoned peremptorily to Sherlock's aid, found her fretful and demanding, arbitrary yet indecisive[64]—and also fully conscious that, like the Professor, she was suffering a decline of her powers. It was indeed time, as she herself recognized, that she abandoned the demanding profession of consulting detective and sought a quieter life.

It is possible that Sherlock was attracted to Mercer, the man whom she took so much trouble to account for to Watson[65]—little though, by then, Watson cared! We consider it certain that she was greatly attracted by the schoolmaster Harold Stackhurst; so much so, perhaps, that her purchase of that cottage on the Sussex Downs was motivated by her desire to be near him (see pp. 108–109). Unfortunately, though the acquaintance ripened for a while, it went sour eventually. Harold was not of an intellectual calibre sufficient to engage Sherlock's interest for long—and besides, he was not Watson. She was by then at that age when one puts away pretence and sees no reason to spend time, for appearance's sake only, with people who are not sufficiently amusing.

For a while Sherlock was content—or forced herself to be content—to concentrate on her bees, writing her treatise on them. This was to be her last and greatest published work—and certainly the one of which she was most proud.

However, these years of rest and recuperation had served to renew her mental strength and energy. At the age of fifty-eight, a time when most other people would be beginning to think of retirement, she was only too willing to give up her tranquility and return to active practice at her country's call. The eminence of the persons who passed on that call must have been especially gratifying to her.[66]

Two adventurous years in the United States followed. Masquerading as the Irish-American secret agent and spy Altamont, Sherlock contrived to infiltrate the German Secret Service. Yet, when she came back to England and was on the threshold of her triumph over the German master-spy Von Bork, she knew only two persons outside Government circles whom she could entirely trust—her aged one-time landlady, Mrs. Hudson, and the steadfast—and, by now, again heart-free—Watson. So it was that these two came to share in Sherlock's greatest triumph.

Perhaps it was not the last occasion on which Watson and she worked together. As we have noted (p. 113), there are hints of a continuing partnership during the bitter years of the Great War.

Nor do we hear any more of Watson and Sherlock; all else is speculation. Were they among the many casualties of that great conflict? Somehow, we do not think so. Afterwards, what happened? Did Sherlock keep up her pretence of masculinity to the very end of her days? Or did she, in old age, find it easier to become Charlotte again, after so long? We believe the latter; and we believe that Watson may well have been persuaded to live with Holmes in that cottage on the Downs.

And the end, when it came—for Sherlock was immortal only in the annals of crime—how was it? It is likely that John Watson died first; men usually do.

What is certain is that, when Sherlock's own time came, no one would trouble to report her death. Who, after all, would heed the passing of an old woman who kept bees upon the Downs of Sussex?[67]

Afterword

Ms. Holmes of Baker Street was born of an early morning telephone call from Bill Sarjeant, who had been jolted out of a deep sleep by one of those things-that-go-click-in-the-night; one of those things that won't leave you alone until you share it with somebody else.

"How would you like to commit the ultimate heresy?" he asked.

"Tell me more," I replied, without—according to Bill—ever pausing to consider the consequences.

His plan was this: each of us would read, notebook at hand, the four novels and fifty-six short stories comprising the Holmes canon, noting and marking any passages that might bolster Bill's lightning-bolt insight that it was not *Watson* who was a woman—as had been playfully suggested by Rex Stout in 1941—but Sherlock Holmes himself.

It sounded simple enough, but at the time we could not have foreseen that we would each crawl through the canon an estimated thirty eye-popping times before our bulging files contained everything we needed to make our case. Nor did we realize that it would take ten years.

What had begun as a more or less lighthearted venture turned quickly serious as the evidence mounted and our files overflowed. Working solely from Sir Arthur Conan Doyle's texts— and having agreed to read none of the Holmes commentators until our own book was complete—we were confronted with literally hundreds of inexplicable instances that could only serve to strengthen our thesis. Frequently we found ourselves having to agree with those earlier writers who had concluded, shaking their heads, that "There's something spooky about Sherlock Holmes."

I won't pretend that it wasn't an uphill battle. One early critic suggested that, given any comparable body of literary material, a similar—perhaps even superior— case could be made for the femininity of its hero. How about *The Odyssey*? Had we used our tools to pry off Homer's hubcaps? Very well, we said, let us apply our methods to Homer. But Ulysses, in spite of our insistent ferreting, remained stubbornly and resolutely male.

What about Conan Doyle's other sustained characters, then? What about Professor Challenger? What about Brigadier Gerard, or Alleyne Edrickson, or Sir Nigel Loring of *The White Company*? Were any of them really women? Not a shred of evidence could we find.

How about Hamlet? No—resoundingly. Lord Peter Wimsey? Sorry: no cigar.

It was Sherlock Holmes and only Sherlock Holmes, when viewed as a male, who gave that curious impression of a person in another room—someone seen reflected in a mirror.

Upon publication, we and our book became something of a *cause célèbre*. Extensive national and international radio and television interviews, newspaper coverage, lectures, book reviews and a public debate made it clear that our readers were left either in warm agreement or cold outrage. There was no middle ground. Although we were shaken at the time, we tended to remember rather fondly in retrospect the elderly lady who attacked us with a wet umbrella in a Toronto supermarket.

"You're the people that think Sherlock Holmes was a woman!" She had seen us on television, and it was clear that we had touched a nerve.

In the years that followed, Ms. Holmes was never far from our minds, and it seemed impossible to go anywhere without meeting someone who had an opinion on the matter. Unlikely encounters and warm discussions became our stock-in-trade, but we somehow managed to strike up many lasting friendships along the way. After all, what harm could come of befriending a couple of old noddies who believed that Sherlock Holmes was a woman?

When it seemed likely that our book was to be republished—and how proud we were that it would published for the first time in Canada—we, and *Ms. Holmes*, began at once preparing to take to the lists once more. Sadly, Bill Sarjeant did not live to see this new edition of *Ms. Holmes of Baker Street* — doubly sad since he had anticipated it with such glee. How oddly and eerily, looking back on it, our final conversation echoed those famous words of Sherlock Holmes to Dr. Watson: "Stand with me here upon the terrace, for it may be the last quiet talk we shall ever have."

Our talk that day was of *Ms. Holmes*, and of our plans for her imminent reappearance on the public stage. Was she up to it? We agreed that she was: that in retrospect we would not change a thing.

And so, in that brief, still moment as she pauses in front of the mirror, eyeing with approval the angle of her deerstalker hat, I would like to take a moment to attend two to pleasant duties: to thank Barbara Roden for her pleasant and perceptive introduction, and to dedicate to the memory of Dr. William A.S. Sarjeant: geologist, teacher, folk-singer, musicologist, broadcaster, novelist, fellow-traveller, co-author and dear friend, this new edition of our little book. Ultimate heresy or not.

Alan Bradley

Kelowna, British Columbia
January 25, 2004

The Dating of the Cases

Discussion

To PLOT THE COURSE OF SHERLOCK HOLMES'S LIFE and to understand his developing relationship with John Watson, it is essential to establish a firm chronology for the adventures recounted in the Canon. We have given this matter prolonged consideration, taking into account the major analyses of the texts by Bell,[1] Brend,[2] Baring-Gould,[3] and Dakin,[4] together with such of the minor writings as have been available to us. The vast volume of Sherlockian scholarship may well mean that some crucial works have eluded us; but we doubt whether these would affect seriously the chronology presented here, if only because that chronology makes such good sense. In particular, it accords with the concept that Watson (during the 19th century, at least) was married once and once only.

Each of the earlier chronologists had his shortcomings. Baring-Gould, for example, placed too much reliance on his phenomenal knowledge of the social history of the period and unwarrantedly expected a precision from Watson of which the doctor was simply not capable. In consequence, he preferred to accept his own deductions on occasion rather than Watson's stated date for a case. Brend, on the other hand, was too kind—too much the gentleman. His preference was for the mellow gaslight of memory, even when it collided with the facts. Dakin's analysis, the latest of the major surveys, has called upon all the earlier ones and seems to us, in many respects, the best and most balanced.

Though, in general, the chronology we have adopted is that of Baring-Gould, we differ from it—and, in most instances, follow Dakin—concerning the dates of seventeen cases, for reasons stated below.

1. The Resident Patient

In the original *Strand Magazine* publication of this case, its timing was indicated with reasonable precision by Watson:

> I cannot be sure of the exact date, for some of my memoranda upon the matter have been mislaid, but it must have been towards the end of the first year during which Holmes and I shared chambers in Baker Street. It was boisterous October weather and we had both remained indoors all day, I because I feared with my shaken health to face the keen autumn wind, while he was deep in some of those abstruse chemical investigations which absorbed him utterly as long as he was engaged upon them.[5]

Despite the arguments advanced by Bell and reiterated by Baring-Gould, we feel this date to be correct. We do not believe Watson would have made the sort of error that they imply, when they transfer the case to 1886. The excision of much of the above-quoted paragraph, when the case was published in book form, was surely a consequence of an over-busy subeditor's removal of what he considered excess verbiage and not, as those two commentators pretend, of Watson's recovery of his notes.

When Watson remembers his own continuing physical weakness after the Maiwand wound[6] and remembers also Holmes's engrossment with chemistry[7]—an interest that faded with the years—he is certainly recollecting a case from the earliest months of their partnership. Thus we discount the supposed evidence to the contrary and adhere to the stated date.

2. The Beryl Coronet

The date allotted by Baring-Gould to this case—Friday, 19th December to Saturday, 20th December, 1890—is unacceptable. Watson was still in residence at Baker Street, whereas in 1890 he would have been married and away. Watson wrote that the case began on "a bright, crisp February morning."[8] Baring-Gould dismissed this statement, since he believed there was no February snowfall during any of the possible years. However, Dr. E.B. Zeisler has demonstrated that there was not only snow in London in 1886, but also that Watson's mentions of morning sunshine and of moonlight at 2 a.m. fit perfectly with February of that year.[9] Like Dakin, we believe the case made by Zeisler to be "cast-iron."[10]

Significantly, this is the only case whose date hinges upon the weather in which Baring-Gould does *not* quote evidence from Zeisler!

3. *The Noble Bachelor*

This case is stated by Watson to have taken place:

> "...a few weeks before my own marriage, during the days when I was
> still sharing rooms with Holmes in Baker Street."[11]

It is also stated that Lord Robert St. Simon was "Born in 1846"[12] and was "forty-one years of age."[13] Provided one assumes that the noble lord had not quite attained his birthday when he consulted Holmes, both dates agree with 1888 as year. Since we do not believe, as did Baring-Gould, that Watson was married twice, we cannot accept his arguments for placing the case into 1886.

We are prepared also, on the basis on the careful reasoning of Dakin,[14] to concur that the case commenced on Friday 12th October.

4. *The Five Orange Pips*

This case was documented by Watson some time after 1890, when he was scanning his notes made between 1882 and that year. With this lapse of time there had come some measure of confusion, for the evidence for the year is contradictory.

Though Watson spends some time in reviewing the array of curious cases that 1887 had brought, he does not state directly that this case dates from that year. Instead, his comment:

> It was in the latter days of September....[15]

begins a separate paragraph. The only fact mentioned that seems to support 1887 is John Openshaw's statement that his father died in January 1885 and 'two years and eight months have elapsed since then.'[16]

The bulk of the evidence strongly favours 1889. First of all, there is a direct reference backward to *A Study in Scarlet*[17] and an indirect one to *A Scandal in Bohemia*, when Holmes admits that he has been beaten four times, three times by men and once by a woman.[18] Furthermore Watson notes:

> My wife was on a visit to her aunt's and for a few days I was a dweller once more in my old quarters at Baker Street.[19]

We consider this conclusive and presume that, when noting Openshaw's statement, Watson had inadvertently changed 'three years' into 'two years.' The meteorological evidence assembled by Zeisler[20] and Christ[21] fixes the commencement of the case as 24th September.

5. The Man with the Twisted Lip

Baring-Gould says succinctly:

> Watson's "June" is accepted by all chronologists, his "'89" by all except your editor, who places the adventure in the June of 1887.[22]

We can only respond, equally succinctly, that we agree with the other chronologists and not with Baring-Gould. In other words, we accept Watson's date for the case.

We can hardly resist mentioning in passing that, had the 1887 date been correct, it would have been surprising that such loyal subjects of Queen Victoria as Holmes and Watson should have failed to mention the 50th Jubilee celebrations. These were to take place on the two days immediately following this case (June 20th and 21st); the streets of London would have been already bedecked with bunting and hung with flags. However, though the adventure took place in the heart of London, no such displays gain mention. A bad slip, Baring-Gould!

6. The Blue Carbuncle

At the time of this case, Watson is married and visiting Holmes not at, but immediately after, Christmas. Baring-Gould places this case into the year 1887, a date acceptable to him in view of his belief that Watson married twice, but not for we who realize that there was only one marriage.

Dakin summarizes the evidence admirably:

> What year? *The Man With the Twisted Lip* is spoken of, so it must be after the summer of 1889; and *The Blue Carbuncle* is not one of the cases assigned to 1890.... It could not be Christmas 1888, which barely covers Watson's marriage; not 1891, when Holmes had disappeared. So December 1889 will be the date.[23]

Whilst we do not agree with Dakin that there were only three cases in 1890, we feel as he does that 1889 is the year. In December 1890, Watson was not in the mood for Holmes's jocular references to Mary Watson's alleged neglect; the problems in their marriage were becoming too serious for jocularity.

7. A Scandal in Bohemia

The date given in Watson's chronicle for this case is 20th March, 1888.[24] This must be assumed to be a typographical error since, as Baring-Gould points out, the 20th of March in that year was a Tuesday, and the case could not have begun on a Tuesday. Moreover, at the time of this case, Watson's marriage was several months old, during which period, as he notes, he had seen little of Holmes.[25] We believe it was the first case after Watson's marriage in which he was involved, which places it firmly into the early months of 1889. It could certainly not have been in 1887 since, in his chronicle of a later adventure, Watson commented that:

> The year 1887 furnished us with a long series of cases....[26]

During such a year, the interval of several months referred to by Watson would have been impossible.

We accept the view advanced by Dakin that the case took place in March, 1889.

8. The Crooked Man and The Engineer's Thumb

Watson states that *The Adventure of the Engineer's Thumb* took place "in the summer of '89, not long after my marriage."[27] He states further that the case of *The Crooked Man* began "one summer night, a few months after my marriage."[28] Both cases, then, took place during the summer of 1889: that, at least, is clear.

Baring-Gould, rather unexpectedly, places both cases into September. This is presumably done to make room for *The Cardboard Box*, which he dates as August 31st to September 2nd, 1889. However, as noted below, we believe that case to have taken place one year earlier. Consequently we do not feel constrained, as he did, to force these two cases into the same late summer month. Nevertheless, we accept his deduction, based on the moon's shining brightly between 1:30 and 2:00 a.m. and having set no later than 3:30 a.m., that the engineer must have lost his thumb on the night of Friday-Saturday, 6th to 7th September.[29]

No such precise evidence is forthcoming for the calendar placement of *The Crooked Man*. However, we are inclined to accept Dakin's reasoning[30] and to place it vaguely into August, 1889.

9. *A Case of Identity*

At the beginning of this case, Watson is visiting Holmes in "his" lodgings at Baker Street.[31] Evidently, therefore, Watson is no longer resident, so the case must succeed his marriage. Consequently the date allocated by Baring-Gould—Tuesday to Wednesday, October 18th to 19th, 1887—is impossible.

To add to the confusion, Holmes notes that the affair of Mary Sutherland—the *Case of Identity*—was "just the other day." Yet, in that case, the printed slip read by Watson stated that Mr. Hosmer Angel went missing 'on the morning of the 14th.'[32]

Moreover, Holmes had recently received his snuff-box from the King of Bohemia,[33] so this case must have post-dated that one—and not by any great interval. Since there was another case in September, 1889, we are inclined to accept Baring-Gould's placement of this investigation into October, especially since the fire burning in Holmes's lodgings[34] indicates that summer was over. (The hardy Victorians would require a very harsh September day indeed before being induced to light a fire!).

10. *The Red-Headed League*

Dakin gives an admirably succinct analysis of the chronological confusion generated by this case:

First we are told at the beginning that [Watson] called on Holmes 'in the autumn of last year' (i.e. 1890, as the story was published in 1891);

then that 27 April was 'just two months ago,' and that it was 'this day eight weeks,' which would mean that it was on a day in June that Wilson the pawnbroker called; and finally that the day of Wilson's consultation was 9 October 1890—at least, that was the day the Red-headed League was dissolved.... To make it worse confounded, it is insisted on several times that the day was Saturday; yet Mr. Bell has pointed out that 9 October 1890 was a Thursday, and the 4th was a Saturday.[35]

It is impossible to formulate a coherent resolution to all these chronological problems; evidently either Watson or the typesetter, or both, blundered badly here. We accept the evidence adduced both by Baring-Gould and by Dakin that the month was October. However, we note that Watson had again "called upon" his friend Holmes,[36] so that Watson was not in residence. Consequently, we feel obliged to follow the consensus of experts, rather than Baring-Gould, by considering 1890 to be the year.

Concerning the month within that year, it is particularly difficult to make a choice. We suggest, rather tentatively, that Watson's 'April' should have read 'August,' which would make Friday 24th and Saturday 25th October, 1890 seem feasible dates for this case.

11. *The Dying Detective*

This case is clearly placed into the second year of Watson's married life, i.e. 1890, and begins on a 'foggy November day.'[37] Since we may be certain that this refers to Watson's marriage to Mary Morstan, we cannot accept Baring-Gould's eclectic conclusion that the case took place in 1887.

12. *The Norwood Builder*

The arguments of Dakin seem conclusive here:

> This must surely be the summer of 1894. Watson states categorically that Holmes had been back for some months, and refers in the next paragraph to 'our months of partnership,' which must mean less than a year; nor could Holmes's complaint that London was a dull place without Moriarty fit any much later time. Holmes's words about 'an August sun on my back' give the month.[38]

13. *Wisteria Lodge*

"Towards the end of March"[39] this case took place; but which March? As Dakin points out cogently:

> ...the year is of all Watson's mistakes the most absurd: he puts 1892, which was in the middle of the Great Hiatus when Holmes was not in London at all, but—wherever he was during the interval. What is the true date? It must be after *The Red-Headed League*, quoted by Holmes at the outset; but the date is really given by the reference in *The Norwood Builder*, which is itself in the summer of 1894, to 'the papers of ex-President Murillo.'[40]

However, we cannot follow Dakin in redating Holmes's return from April to February 1894. We are forced to conclude that Watson made a double error—not only in the year, but also in the month.

The bleak and windy weather is not characteristic of any particular month; in England, such weather can happen in *any* month. (The second author has endured bleak weather on the Sussex coast even in early July!) The quarter day could be that of June—Midsummer Day (24th)—rather than that of March—Lady Day (25th). This fits better with Eccles's statement that "quarter day is at hand."[41] Since, in *late* March, the quarter day would be past! We consider, therefore, that the adventure took place either in late May or mid-June 1894. However, we are unprepared to speculate upon the exact days, for want of conclusive evidence.

14. *The Disappearance of Lady Frances Carfax*

This is a very difficult case to date with any precision and, once again, we find Dakin's arguments more persuasive than those of Baring-Gould. Dakin writes:

> ...it was after the Return: Holy Peters' ear was bitten in a saloon fight in 1889, which means the story is 1891 or later.... But after 1891 we have any year to pick from. I might choose 1899 for no better reason than that we have no other cases recorded for it after *Charles Augustus Milverton* in January. That Watson was feeling rheumatic and old really gives us no clue. But Dr. Theodore Gibson has made the ingenious point that Holmes had the telephone installed by 1898 (the date of

The Retired Colourman), and if he had possessed it when Lady Frances was in such imminent danger of being buried alive he would have surely used it to get someone else to Poultney Square more quickly than he could manage it. By this argument we should have to put Lady Frances in 1897 or earlier.[42]

As Dakin notes also, the fact that Holy Peters spent his time in a lounge chair on the verandah indicates a summer month. We are prepared, therefore, to accept Baring-Gould's argument for a July date.

15. *The Hound of the Baskervilles*

This is one of two cases which Baring-Gould places between *The Sign of the Four*, when Watson met Mary Morstan, and *The Boscombe Valley Mystery*, when they are first mentioned as having entered the state of, we fear, all-too-temporary connubial bliss. We cannot accept his placement of those cases.

Yet, at first examination, Baring-Gould's reasoning appears impeccable. Dr. Mortimer's stick, we are told, bore the date 1884. Not only that, but five dates are given (from 1882 to 1884) which, we are further told, occur in Dr. Mortimer's record in the Medical Directory. Since Holmes states unequivocally that the date on the stick was "five years ago,"[43] the year seems to be fixed as 1889.

However, in this case we believe that Brend's conclusions outweigh even the printed evidence. As he points out, is it reasonable to imagine that Watson would have made no mention of his fiancee *at any time* during this quite lengthy chronicle and would not even have written to her from Dartmoor?[44] That article on "Free Trade" in *The Times*, used to furnish the warning to Sir Henry Baskerville, could never have appeared in 1889, a year when free trade was not a political issue. Finally, in 1889 Lestrade was most certainly not treating Holmes with the reverence he showed in *The Hound!* We agree with Brend that the fault must again be laid with that officious subeditor who, having misread Watson's handwriting and changed 1899 into 1889, thereafter proceeded to "logicalize" the rest of the text by altering the Medical Directory dates also. In every respect, 1899 seems the proper year for this case.

16. *The Cardboard Box*

This case is mentioned in *The Sign of the Four*, which we know to have taken place in September 1888. Despite Baring-Gould's ingenious arguments from meteorological data and the sittings of Parliament, his placement of the case after *The Sign* is simply not acceptable. We believe, therefore, that it commenced "on a blazing day of August"[45] 1888, not 1889.

Nor can we accept the dates August 31st to September 2nd. Had the day been the last in August, would not Watson have remarked upon the fact? An unspecified "day of August" is surely not likely to have been the last day of the month!

17. *The Copper Beeches*
In dating this adventure, Baring-Gould again places himself out on a limb:

> All chronologists except your editor would seem to agree that Watson was married at the time of this adventure. This presents them with a difficulty, since Watson is here completely silent about a wife or professional duties and appears to be living in Baker Street, not for a few days only, but for the entire fortnight covered by the adventure. In our view, the adventure was the last shared by the doctor and the detective before Watson's marriage to Mary Morstan circa May 1, 1889.[46]

We cannot accept this deduction. Watson refers to the "old room in Baker Street,"[47] a phrase which (as Brend percipiently notes) would not have been used had he been still living there. It is clear that, having been away, he had returned to the familiar quarters. The absence of any reference to a wife with whom, by then, there was a developing estrangement is less remarkable than would have been the absence of reference to a fiancee to whom Watson felt a passionate attachment.

The reference to five earlier cases[48] is also helpful. The latest of these, *The Man with the Twisted Lip*, is (as we have noted above) explicitly dated to June 1889. This particular case must have taken place at a later time, after the marriage. All in all, the evidence favours Brend's 1890 dating.[49]

18. *The Dancing Men* and *The Retired Colourman*
According to Baring-Gould's chronology, the dates for these cases overlapped. For the first, he quotes 27th July to 13th August 1898; for the second, 28th to 30th July 1898.

As Baring-Gould points out, only one of the two years is possible. The evidence for this is furnished by Mr. Hilton Cubitt's statement:

"Last year I came up to London for the Jubilee."[50]

The year therefore must be either 1888 or 1898 and Baring-Gould's scrutiny of dates supports the latter.

The date for the second case can be established equally satisfactorily as 1898, since it is "within two years" of Josiah Amberley's marriage "early 1897."[51]

However, there is no real reason to suppose that the cases overlapped and every reason to assume that they did not. Indeed, three cases are involved; did not Holmes express his inability to accompany Watson to Lewisham because of his preoccupation with the affair of the two Coptic Patriarchs?[52]

It is technically conceivable that, after the interview with Mr. Cubitt, Holmes might have set that other matter aside for two days while he dealt with the odious Amberley. And yet, during the affair of the Dancing Men, we find Watson writing as follows:

…Several times in the next few days I saw [Holmes] take his slip of paper from his notebook and look long and earnestly at the curious figures inscribed upon it.[53]

Had Holmes been involved in the affairs both of Amberley and of the Patriarchs, he would scarcely have had leisure for such contemplation.

No, the cases cannot have overlapped; they must have been separated at least by a few days. It is conceivable that the affair of the Retired Colourman took place in June or early July, as Brend suggests;[54] but the fact that Amberley's garden was "all running to seed"[55] indicates a time in late summer. Thus we assign a late August date to this case.

In the remaining cases of the canon, Baring-Gould's reasoning and his chronology seem to us perfectly acceptable and to be in good accord with Holmes's and Watson's developing character and relationships, as they adventured, loved and grew old, apart or together.

Chronology

GLOR	*The Gloria Scott*	15th July to 22nd September 1873
MUSG	*The Musgrave Ritual*	2nd October 1879
STUD	*A Study in Scarlet*	4th to 7th March 1881
RESI	*The Resident Patient*	6th October 1882
SPEC	*The Speckled Band*	6th to 7th April 1883
BERY	*The Beryl Coronet*	23rd to 24th February 1886
SECO	*The Second Stain*	12th to 15th October 1886
REIG	*The Reigate Squires*	14th to 26th April 1887
VALL	*The Valley of Fear*	7th to 8th January 1888
YELL	*The Yellow Face*	7th April 1888
CARD	*The Cardboard Box*	August 1888
GREE	*The Greek Interpreter*	12th September 1888
SIGN	*The Sign of the Four*	18th to 21st September 1888
NOBL	*The Noble Bachelor*	12th October 1888
SCAN	*A Scandal in Bohemia*	20th to 22nd March 1889
BOSC	*The Boscombe Valley Mystery*	8th to 9th June 1889
STOC	*The Stockbroker's Clerk*	15th June 1889
TWIS	*The Man with the Twisted Lip*	Late June 1889
NAVA	*The Naval Treaty*	30th July to 1st August 1889
CROO	*The Crooked Man*	Summer 1889
ENGR	*The Engineer's Thumb*	7th to 8th September 1889
FIVE	*The Five Orange Pips*	24th to 25th September 1889
IDEN	*A Case of Identity*	18th to 19th October 1889
BLUE	*The Blue Carbuncle*	27th December 1889
COPP	*The Copper Beeches*	5th to 20th April 1890
SILV	*Silver Blaze*	25th and 30th September 1890
REDH	*The Red-Headed League*	24th to 25th October 1890
DYIN	*The Dying Detective*	19th November 1890
FINA	*The Final Problem*	24th April to 4th May 1891
EMPT	*The Empty House*	5th April 1894
WIST	*Wisteria Lodge*	Six days in May or June 1894
NORW	*The Norwood Builder*	August 1894
GOLD	*The Golden Pince-Nez*	14th to 15th November 1894
3STU	*The Three Students*	5th to 6th April 1895
SOLI	*The Solitary Cyclist*	13th to 20th April 1895
BLAC	*Black Peter*	3rd to 5th July 1895
BRUC	*The Bruce-Partington Plans*	21st to 23rd November 1895

VEIL	*The Veiled Lodger*	October 1896
SUSS	*The Sussex Vampire*	19th to 21st November 1896
MISS	*The Missing Three-Quarter*	8th to 10th December 1896
ABBE	*Abbey Grange*	23rd January 1897
DEVI	*The Devil's Foot*	16th to 20th March 1897
LADY	*The Disappearance of Lady Frances Carfax*	1st to 18th July 1897
DANC	*The Dancing Men*	27th July to 10th August and 13th August 1898
RETI	*The Retired Colourman*	Late August 1898
CHAS	*Charles Augustus Milverton*	5th to 14th January 1899
HOUN	*The Hound of the Baskervilles*	26th September to 20th October 1899
SIXN	*The Six Napoleons*	8th to 10th June 1900
THOR	*The Problem of Thor Bridge*	4th to 5th October 1900
PRIO	*The Priory School*	16th to 18th May 1901
SHOS	*Shoscombe Old Place*	6th to 7th May 1902
3GAR	*The Three Garridebs*	26th to 27th June 1902
ILLU	*The Illustrious Client*	3rd to 16th September 1902
REDC	*The Red Circle*	Between November 1902 and March 1903
BLAN	*The Blanched Soldier*	7th to 12th January 1903
3GAB	*The Three Gables*	26th to 27th May 1903
MAZA	*The Mazarin Stone*	Summer 1903
CREE	*The Creeping Man*	6th, 14th and 22nd September 1903
LION	*The Lion's Mane*	27th July to 3rd August 1909
LAST	*His Last Bow*	2nd August 1914

APPENDIX II

Clues By Cryptogram?

IT IS TEMPTING TO ANALYZE the name adopted by our heroine in quest for hidden indications of her identity or concealed proclamations of her femininity. Y. Nakagawa (1980, *Holmes wa onna datta*, Tokyo: Hayakawa Shobo, 180 p.) suggested that she may have chosen her name in anticipation of the fashion in which letters would be addressed to her. He pointed out that, in the formal style of the epoch, all polite communications by mail would be inscribed to "Sherlock Holmes, Esq."—initials that spell SHE. With even greater ingenuity, Mr. Nakagawa proceeded to construct an arrangement of the titles to try to discover her name and decided that their initial letters spelled out MARY HOLMES— but this procedure, we feel, is too arbitrary and improbable to be acceptable.

Much more appealing to us is the approach set forth in a letter to the second author from an English friend, Mrs. Monica Dobbs of Sheffield, who was wholly unfamiliar with Nakagawa's ideas. She wrote as follows:

> Sherlock Holmes—take the first three letters and what have we got? S-H-E. Move along one and again take the three letters—that gives us H-E-R. Move along one again and discover E-R-L!! Now what do we make of that? Stand back and take another look at that name. What is this person doing to us? Remove those three letters from the name and we are left in a state of S-H-O-C-K.

So—we move on to the surname—but, although tempted, we can't apply the same rules there—a surname is not so specific. It's a lovely mixture of male and female, we see—neatly interlaced—LE and MS. What do you make of that, my dear? I'd say a cunning mind indeed. We are left with these two remaining letters and I do believe this—this *person*—has had the last laugh on all of us—HO! HO!

There we have it—the whole name—just like the Secret Letter that was propped against the clock on the mantel-piece—[it] has been staring everyone in the face all along.

The "Secret Letter" is of course, the "Purloined Letter" of Edgar Allan Poe's famous story.

Mrs. Dobbs comments on her interpretation as follows:

But it's still a bit of an enigma—constructed around those letters ERL—a genius, devilish, tantalizing, cunning. There's a female mind at work there. 'Logic' would argue—and could argue—otherwise; and yet, and yet. "Frailty, thy name is...." "She" wanted to be discovered—and admired—eventually, otherwise there would have been no fun in it.... That name can be considered, now, in two ways:

a. It's a statement of fact concerning the person's sex.

b. It's an enigma, cunningly contrived. Is it, in fact, a code at all? There's just enough to attract your attention and now this person is leading you off on a merry chase (typically female?) "She's" got all your attention. She's subtle and she's clever and the chase is going to be interesting.

With that last comment, we could not agree more!

The mind that could while away its time deciphering original inscriptions on palimpsests was surely capable of such cryptonymic ingenuities!

APPENDIX III

Biorhythms and the Birthday

DURING THE WRITING OF THIS BOOK, the authors have had many opportunities to ponder and discuss cyclical aspects in the make-up of Sherlock Holmes. Time and again our researches have been tempted away from the main thesis— temptations that we trust, for the most part, we have overcome.

There is one area, however, which we felt deserving of more attention, and one without which our study would be less than complete: that of the pseudo-science known as the study of biorhythmicity. This we have included separately from the main body of the text for two reasons: first, because we felt that the unproven nature of the evidence for biorhythms might jeopardize the credibility of an otherwise serious work of scholarship, and second, because this matter, with its charts and digressions, would interrupt the flow of our more crucial evidences of Holmes's femininity.

Let us being with a rapid overview of biorhythms. Although humans had noted throughout recorded history the ups-and-downs of individual behaviour, the subject seems to have evaded serious study until the latter half of the nine-teenth century when a German physician, Wilhelm Fliess, published a formula for biological rhythms. He had found that children were prone to illness at regular intervals. For twenty years he collected data on thousands of people, charting the ups and downs of their lives—accidents, illnesses, marriage, divorce, pay raises, or being fired from a job. The chart lines formed waves rising and

falling regularly through the months.[1] Of his work, it is particularly interesting
in a Sherlockian context to note the use of cocaine, which Fliess applied to what
he termed "penital cells" within his patients' nostrils, for Fliess believed neurotic
symptoms and sexual abnormalities to be related to nasal irritation!

By 1897 Fliess had been joined in that field of study by Hermann Swoboda.
From the researches of both men came the observation that each of us contains
not one, but three distinct sets of waves representing our emotional, physical
and mental indicators.[2] These waves were thought to have repetition rates of
twenty-three, twenty-eight, and thirty-three days respectively. The waves began
with a value of zero on the day of one's birth and continued throughout life,
rising and falling with those three aspects of one's condition. It is only a simple
calculation to show that these repetitions will move into phase in one's twenty-
seventh year, and again in one's twenty-ninth year. Further, all three waves will
reset to zero and begin again, immediately following a major conjunction of
three zero-crossings, shortly after one's fifty-eighth birthday.

Each day when each cycle crossed the zero axis in passing from positive to
negative, or vice versa, was called a "critical" day[3] and was thought to be a time
when one was particularly susceptible to breakdown in terms of that particular
physical, emotional, or mental wave-crossing.

From time to time, these wave passages across the zero axis would coincide
when two, or even three of the indicators would make a crossing on the same
day. These triply critical days were thought to form the major crises of one's life.
It was believed by some[4] that a careful study of one's "critical" days could serve
as a divination of one's destiny.

By the same token, we reasoned, it should be possible to work backwards
from the dates of known events to find a birthday, and to verify other "critical"
coincidences while on the way.

We began by taking the usually accepted birthdate of Sherlock Holmes,
January 6th, 1854, and feeding this into a computerized biorhythm program.
It was necessary to establish a "check-point"—a well-known date of physical,
emotional and mental breakdown. In addition, it was necessary to find a specific
date that was agreed upon by all the many Holmes chronologists. The choice
was an easy one: that date given so definitely by Watson at the beginning of the
Reigate Squires:

> It was some time before the health of my friend, Mr. Sherlock
> Holmes, recovered from the strain caused by his immense exertions in
> the spring of [18]'87....

On referring to my notes, I see that it was on the 14th of April that I received a telegram from Lyons, which informed me that Holmes was lying ill in the Hotel Dulong.[5]

Watson tells us that his iron constitution had broken down

...under the strain of an investigation which had extended over two months, during which period he had never worked less than fifteen hours a day, and had more than once, as he assured me, kept to his task for five days at a stretch.[6]

It seems a reasonable assumption to make that Watson was informed immediately by Sherlock of her breakdown. No continental hotel would want to be solely responsible for the welfare of a foreign woman who had fallen ill in her travels. That Holmes's French cousins the Vernets were informed seems improbable; if such had been the case, there would have been no cause for Sherlock to send that telegram seeking Watson's help. There is also the fact that Watson tells us it was three days before they were back in Baker Street;[7] a comment which could only mean that he was forced to wait a full day in France before Sherlock was deemed fit to travel. We can scarcely believe that Watson would wait a day in England before going to her rescue.

Therefore, it is likeliest that Sherlock's breakdown took place on Thursday, the 14th of April, while Wednesday the 13th would be the very earliest possible date. These were the dates with which we began our search.

It can be seen that the Holmes biorhythm, based on the January 6th, 1854 birthdate, shows no critical passage on that date (Figure 1).

The only doubly critical crossing seems to fall, not on April 15th but on April 7th, 1887, when the physical and intellectual waves both pass through zero.

From this conjunction, only three possibilities of interpretation exist. The first is that Watson erred in reporting April 14th, 1887 as the date on which he received word of Holmes's breakdown, when in fact it had occurred either a week earlier or else in some other year.

The second possibility is that Holmes's true birthday was other than January 6th. Setting that critical crossing of Holmes's physical and emotional well-being on April 14, 1887, as Watson has reported, we work back to find that a birthdate of January 13th, 1854 may be the correct one. The result can be clearly seen in Figure 2.

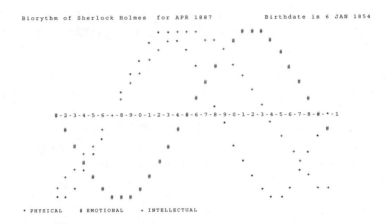

Figure 1

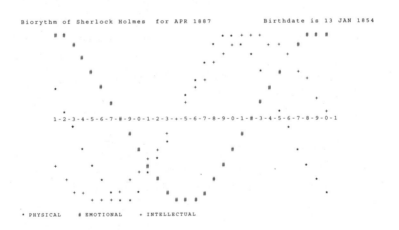

Figure 2

This finding seems to us to be reasonable enough. Earlier commentators on the canon have set the January 6th date on the grounds that Twelfth Night seemed an appropriate date for Sherlock's birth. This was supported by a deduction made by Nathan L. Bengis. He noted that, in the case chronicled as *The Valley of Fear*, Holmes,

> ...leaned upon his hand, with his untouched breakfast before him...[8]

> "Surely it is clear," Mr. Bengis wrote, "that there had been some small jollification the night before in celebration of the Master's birthday, and that his lack of appetite was the result of a hangover?"[9]

This seems to us an overly slender basis for such a major conclusion! We have no least indication from the chronicles that Sherlock ever drank to excess—and, on our particular thesis, it was a risk she could never afford to take.

While it has not been our intent here to carry out a complete analysis of Holmesian critical dates through the use of biorhythms, we believe that further consideration of those conjunctions will prove a rewarding field of study for the interested investigator.

$\mathcal{N}otes$

Foreword

1   A. Bradley and W.A.S. Sarjeant, "The Woman," *From the Mantelpiece*, no. 4, 4 unnum. p.

2   B.D. Kennedy, "Cherchez La Femme," in W.J. Walsh, ed., *A Curious Collection* (Suffern, N.Y.: The Musgrave Ritualists Beta), 19–22.

3   C. Davies, "A Scandal in Baker Street," *The Guardian*, 30 March 1974. [Also publ. in *Sherlockiana*, 19.2–3 (1974), 10–11 and in *Sherlock Holmes Journal*, 11.4 (1974): 124–26.]

4   E. Sorkin, "Heresy," *Sherlockian Meddler*, 7.4 (1979): 30–32.

5   Y. Nakagawa, *Holmes wa onna datta* (Tokyo: Hayakawa Shobo, 1980).

Chapter One

1   D.M. Dakin, *A Sherlock Holmes Commentary* (Newton Abbot, Devon, England: David & Charles, 1972), 277–78.

2   Dakin, *A Sherlock Holmes Commentary*, 277.

3   R. Stout, "Watson Was a Woman," *The Saturday Review of Literature*, 23.19 (1941): 3–4, 16.

4   Eight instances may be adduced:

"You know my methods in such cases, Watson." MUSG (I, 137)

"You know my methods of work...." VALL (I, 511)

"My dear fellow, you know my methods." STOCK (II, 154)

"You know my methods. Apply them...." SIGN (I, 638)

"You know my methods. Apply them!" HOUN (I, 5)

"You know my methods, Watson." CROO (II, 230)

"You know my methods." BLUE (I, 453)

"You know my method." BOSC (II, 148)

5   GLOR (I, 107)

6   MUSG (I, 137)

7   REDH (I, 438)

8   SCAN (I, 358)

9   COPP (II, 115)

10 EMPT (II, 340)

11 STUD (I, 151)

12 STUD (I, 153)

13 GLOR (I, 107)

14 I. McQueen, *Sherlock Holmes Detected* (Newton Abbot: David & Charles, 1974).

15 HOUN (II, 110)

16 3GAB (II, 728)

17 SIGN (I, 611)

18 STUD (I, 174)

19 STUD (I, 174)

20 STUD (I, 160)

21 DYIN (I, 450)

22 STUD (I, 153)

23 VEIL (II, 453)

24 REDC (II, 691)

25 LION (II, 782)

26 SIGN (I, 661)

27 HOUN (II, 82)

28 BLAN (II, 716)

29 MUSG (I, 123)

Chapter Two

1   STUD (I, 156)

2   STUD (I, 156)

3   Dakin, *A Sherlock Holmes Commentary*, 17.

4   GLOR (I, 107)

5   GLOR (I, 107)

6   GLOR (I, 108)

7   GLOR (I, 108)

8   SHOS (II, 638)

9   STUD (I, 151)

10   For contrary opinions, see D.L. Sayers, "Holmes' College Career," in H.W. Bell, ed.,
      Baker Street Studies (London: Constable, 1934), 1–34, and G. Brend, *My Dear*
      Holmes, A Study in Sherlock (London: Allen and Unwin, 1951), 18–28.

11   MUSG (I, 126)

12   STOC (II, 153)

13   VALL (I, 514)

14   MUSG (I, 126)

15   MUSG (I, 125)

16   MUSG (I, 125)

17   M. Harrison, *The London of Sherlock Holmes* (Newton Abbot, Devon: David &
      Charles, 1972): 11.

Chapter Three

1   STUD (I, 148)

2   STUD (I, 149)

3   STUD (I, 148)

4   STUD (I, 153)

5   STUD (I, 150)

6   STUD (I, 178)

7   CARD (II, 193–94)

8   CARD (II, 194–95)

9   SPEC (I, 243)

10   SPEC (I, 243)

11   J.E. Holroyd "The Egg Spoon," *Sherlock Holmes Journal*, 1.1 (1952): 24–26.

12   SPEC (I, 244)

13   SPEC (I, 243)

14   SPEC (I, 252)

15   SPEC (I, 256–57)

16   BERY (II, 294–95)

17   BERY (II, 295)

18   BERY (II, 295)

19   MUSG (I, 124)

20   BERY (II, 294–95)

21   BERY (II, 295)

22   BERY (II, 295)

23   BERY (II, 297)

24   SECO (I, 311)

25   SECO (I, 311)

26   SECO (I, 310)

27   SECO (I, 311)

28   SECO (I, 313)

Chapter Four

1   REIG (II, 331)

2   REIG (II, 331)

3   REIG (II, 331)

4   REIG (II, 340)

5   VALL (I, 481)

6   VALL (I, 481)

7   VALL (I, 506)

8   VALL (I, 506)

9   VALL (I, 514)

10 VALL (I, 510)

11 VALL (I, 514)

12 YELL (I, 575)

13 YELL (I, 575)

14 YELL (I, 589)

15 YELL (I, 589)

16 CARD (II, 201)

17 MUSG (I, 123)

18 STUD (I, 173)

19 BOSC (II, 148), STUD (I, 173), SIGN (I, 612)

20 GREE (I, 601)

21 GREE (I, 593)

22 GREE (I, 593)

23 GREE (I, 602)

24 R.K. Leavitt, "Annie Oakley in Baker Street," in E.W. Smith, ed., *Profile by Gaslight* (New York: Simon & Schuster, 1944): 230–42.

25 S. McMillan and G. James, "The Guns of Sherlock Holmes," *Guns & Ammo*, (April 1975): 50–53, 83.

26 SIGN (I, 619)

27 SIGN (I, 619)

28 SIGN (I, 619)

29 SIGN (I, 687)

30 SIGN (I, 688)

31 SIGN (I, 688)

32 NOBL (I, 281)

33 NOBL (I, 281)

34 NOBL (I, 284)

35 NOBL (I, 285)

36 NOBL (I, 292)

37 NOBL (I, 300)

38 NOBL (I, 300)

Chapter Five

1   SCAN (I, 346–47)

2   SCAN (I, 348)

3   SCAN (I, 348)

4   SCAN (I, 348–49)

5   SCAN (I, 367)

6   SCAN (I, 365)

7   SCAN (I, 366)

8   BOSC (II, 134)

9   BOSC (II, 134)

10   BOSC (II, 134)

11   BOSC (II, 134)

12   BOSC (II, 136)

13   BOSC (II, 137)

14   STOC (II, 153–54)

15   ENGI (II, 209)

16   TWIS (I, p. 369)

17   D.L. Sayers, "Dr. Watson's Christian Name," in E.W. Smith, ed., *Profile by Gaslight* (New York: Simon & Schuster, 1944), 180–86.

18   G. Playfair, "John and James," *Baker Street Journal*, new ser., 5.2 (1946): 121.

19   R.S. Katz, "Mary Morstan Moriarty," *Baker Street Journal*, new ser., 27.1, 22–23.

20   A.C. Simpson, "It Must Have Been Two Other Fellows," *Leaves from the Copper Beeches* (Narberth, Pa: Livingston Publishing Co., 1959), 41–53.

21   TWIS (I, 369)

22   TWIS (I, 368)

23   B. Davies, "Holmes and the Halls," *Sherlock Holmes Journal*, 7.3 (1965): 68–73.
     R. Pearson, "A Scandal in Kent," *Serpentine Muse*, 6.1 (1981): 4–12.
     C. Redmond, *In Bed with Sherlock Holmes* (Toronto: Simon & Pierre, 1984), 95.

24   TWIS (I, 382)

25   NAVA (II, 191)

26   CROO (II, 225)

27   ENGI (II, 209)

28   ENGI (II, 210)

29   FIVE (I, 390)

30   FIVE (I, 396)

31   FIVE (I, 399)

32   FIVE (I, 402)

33   FIVE (I, 402)

34   SCAN (I, 367)

35   IDEN (I, 405)

36   IDEN (I, 405)

37   BRUC (II, 452)

38   IDEN (I, 416)

39   BLUE (I, 454)

40   COPP (II, 115)

41   COPP (II, 132)

42   COPP (II, 114)

43   SILV (II, 281)

44   SILV (II, p. 272: it is virtually reiterated on 281)

45   REDH (I, 418)

46   REDH (I, 431)

47   REDH (I, 431–32)

48   SIGN (I, 667)

49   MUSG (I, 123)

50   REDH (I, 438)

51   REDH (I, 438)

52   DYIN (I, 439)

53   DYIN (I, 440)

54   DYIN (I, 449)

55   DYIN (I, 439)

56   DYIN (I, 450)

57   DYIN (I, 450)

58   FINA (II, 301)

59   FINA (II, 302)

60   FINA (II, 302)

61   FINA (II, 302)

Chapter Six

1   EMPT (II, 336–37)

2   J. Tracey, *The Encyclopaedia Sherlockiana; or, A Universal Dictionary of the State of Knowledge of Sherlock Holmes and his Biographer John H. Watson, M.D.* (New York: Doubleday, 1977), 144.

3   EMPT (II, 333)

4   Dakin, *A Sherlock Holmes Commentary*, 156.

5   Examples are P. Heldenbrand, "The Duplicity of Sherlock Holmes," in *Two Baker Street Akronisms* (Summit, New Jersey: The Pamphlet House, 1945), 7–11 and D. Henderson, "No Sich Person," *Sherlock Holmes Journal*, 7.3 (1965), 93–94. Note also the development of this theme in N. Meyer, *The Seven-Per-Cent Solution. Being a Reprint from the Reminiscences of John H. Watson, M.D.* (New York: Dutton, 1974).

6   VALL (I, 477–80)

7   EMPT (II, 333)

8   GLOR (I, 107, 109)

9   GLOR (I, 108)

10   EMPT (II, 342)

11   EMPT (II, 342–43)

12   EMPT (II, 343)

13   W.S. Baring-Gould, *Sherlock Holmes of Baker Street. A Biography of the World's First Consulting Detective* (London: Hart-Davis, 1962), 175–79. A rebuttal is to be found in B.D. Kennedy, "The Truth about Nero Wolfe," *Baker Street Journal*, old ser. 18.3 (1967): 154–55.

14   For an extreme reaction see A. Boucher, "Was the Later Holmes an Imposter?" in E.W. Smith, ed., *Profile by Gaslight* (New York: Simon & Schuster, 1944), 60–70.

Chapter Seven

1   EMPT (II, 337)

2   WIST (II, 238)

3   WIST (II, 239)

4   EMPT (II, 333)

5   WIST (II, 238)

6   WIST (II, 250)

7   WIST (II, 239)

8   WIST (II, 240–41)

9   WIST (II, 241)

10   WIST

11   WIST

12   WIST (II, 245)

13   NORW (II, 414)

14   NORW (II, 414)

15   NORW (II, 414)

16   GOLD (II, 350)

17   GOLD (II, 351)

18   GOLD (II, 361)

19   3STU (II, 368)

20   3STU (II, 369)

21   SOLI (II, 384)

22   SOLI (II, 390)

23   SOLI (II, 391)

24   SOLI (II, 394)

25   BLAC (II, 410)

26   BLAC (II, 399)

27   BRUC (II, 433)

28   BRUC (II, 447)

29 BRUC (II, 452)

30 VEIL (II, 461)

31 M. Howell and P. Ford, *The True History of the Elephant Man* (New York: Allison & Busby, 1980), 128.

32 SUSS (II, 474)

33 MISS (II, 477–78)

34 MISS (II, 483)

35 MISS (II, 487)

36 MISS (II, 487)

37 MISS (II, 479)

Chapter Eight

1 ABBE (II, 491)

2 *Ibid.* (II, 503)

3 ABBE (II, 491)

4 ABBE (II, 492) We may note that Holmes here echoes—or, perhaps, mocks—that famous retort of James McNeill Whistler. When Oscar Wilde, impressed by one of Whistler's sallies, commented "I wish I had said that!," Whistler responded: "You will, Oscar, you will!"

5 DEVI (II, 508)

6 DEVI (II, 508)

7 DEVI (II, 520)

8 DEVI (II, 525)

9 LADY (II, 661)

10 LADY (II, 661)

11 LADY (II, 656–57)

12 W.S. Baring-Gould has made this same deduction as his footnote (656) makes evident.

13 LADY (II, 669)

14 DANC (II, 528)

15 M. Harrison, *In the Footsteps of Sherlock Holmes.*

16 RETI (II, 546)

17 RETI (II, 546)

18 RETI (II, 547)

19 RETI (II, 546)

20 CHAS (II, 562)

21 CHAS (II, 563)

22 CHAS (II, 564)

23 CHAS (II, 562)

24 CHAS (II, 567)

25 HOUN (II, 15)

26 HOUN (II, 35)

27   HOUN (II, 82)

28   HOUN (II, 83)

29   HOUN (II, 83)

30   HOUN (II, 103)

31   SIXN (II, 574)

32   SIXN (II, 583)

33   SIXN (II, 585)

34   THOR (II, 589)

35   THOR (II, 589)

36   THOR (II, 589)

37   THOR (II, 591)

38   THOR (II, 592)

39   THOR (II, 595)

40   THOR (II, 601)

41   THOR (II, 605)

42   THOR (II, 605)

43   PRIO (II, 604)

44   *As You Like It*, Act II, Scene vii.

45   PRIO (II, 612)

46   SHOS (II, 630)

47   SILV (II, 261–81)

48   SHOS (II, 630)

49   SHOS (II, 635)

50   S.R. Meaker, "Watson Medicus," *The Third Cab* (Boston, Mass.: The Speckled Band, 1960) 27–37.

51   3GAR (II, 643)

52   BRUC (II, 452)

53   GOLD (II, 350)

54   3GAR (II, 654)

Chapter Nine

1   ILLU (II, 672)

2   G.R. Sims, ed., *Living London* (London: Cassell, 1901): 370.

3   ILLU (II, 671)

4   ILLU (II, 671)

5   ILLU (II, 684)

6   ILLU (II, 676)

7   ILLU (II, 673)

8   ILLU (II, 683)

9   ILLU (II, 684)

10   ILLU (II, 684)

11   REDC (II, 691)

12   REDC (II, 694)

13   SCAN (I, 356)

14   See Baring-Gould's notes (II, 698) and Dakin, *A Sherlock Holmes Commentary*, 249–57.

15   Dakin, *A Sherlock Holmes Commentary*, 249.

16   BLAN (II, 707)

17   EMPT (II, 337)

18   TWIS (I, 378, 381)

19   BLAN (II, 715)

20   BLAN (II, 707)

21   BLAN (II, 707)

22   BLAN (II, 707)

23   BLAN (II, 720)

24   Dakin, *A Sherlock Holmes Commentary*, 249.

25   3GAB (II, 722)

26   3GAB (II, 728)

27   3GAB (II, 724)

28   3GAB (II, 725)

29   3GAB (II, 728)

30   3GAB (II, 728–29)

31   3GAB (II, 730)

32   3GAB (II, 730)

33   3GAB (II, 731)

34   3GAB (II, 729)

35   3GAB (II, 733)

36   3GAB (II, 733)

37   3GAB (II, 733)

38   3GAB (II, 733)

39   3GAB (II, 733)

40   3GAB (II, 733)

41   3GAB (II, 733)

42   MAZA (II, 735)

43   MAZA (II, 735)

44   MAZA (II, 737, 740)

45   MAZA (II, 737)

46   MAZA (II, 735)

47   MAZA (II, 736)

48   MAZA (II, 736)

49   MAZA (II, 737)

50   MAZA (II, 747)

51   CREE (II, 751)

52 CREE (II, 752)

53 CREE (II, 757)

54 CREE (II, 760)

55 CREE (II, 760)

56 CREE (II, 761)

57 CREE (II, 761)

58 CREE (II, 760–61)

59 CREE (II, 761)

60 CREE (II, 751)

61 CREE (II, 765)

62 CREE (II, 763)

Chapter Ten

1   LION (II, 776)

2   LION (II, 776)

3   LION (II, 776)

4   CREE (II, 763)

5   LION (II, 781)

6   LION (II, 781–82)

7   LION (II, 787)

8   LION (II, 789)

9   LION (II, 784)

10 STUD (I, 154)

11 N.L. Bengis, "Sherlock Stays After School," in J.N. Williamson, ed., *The Illustrious Clients' Second Case-Book* (Indianapolis, Ind.: The Illustrious Clients, 1949), 72–78.

12 LION (II, 785)

13 LION (II, 777)

14 LION (II, 776)

15 LION (II, 789)

16 LION (II, 784)

17 VEIL (II, 453)

18 LAST (II, 797)

19 LAST (II, 800)

20 LAST (II, 800)

21 S.C. Roberts, *Dr. Watson: Prolegomena to the Study of a Biographical Problem, with a Bibliography of Sherlock Holmes* (London: Faber & Faber, 1931).

22 LAST (II, 803)

23 Roberts, *Dr. Watson.*

24 LAST (II, 792)

25 LAST (II, 796)

26   LAST (II, 793)

27   LAST (II, 803)

28   LAST (II, 800)

29   STUD (I, 159)

30   SIGN (I, 612)

31   BRUC (II, 449)

Chapter Eleven

1   The first—R.B. De Waal, *The World Bibliography of Sherlock Holmes and Dr. Watson. A Classified and Annotated List of Materials Relating to their Lives and Adventures* (New York: Bramhall House, 1974) contains over 6,000 entries, while the companion volume—R.B. De Waal, *The International Sherlock Holmes* (Hamden, Conn.: Archon Books, 1980)—adds a further 6,000. Mr. De Waal has informed us that a second supplement is in active preparation.

2   N. Meyer, *The Seven-Per-Cent Solution.*

3   "The Private Life of Sherlock Holmes," (England: Mirisch Films, 1970). A book version of the film exists also: M. and M. Hardwick, *The Private Life of Sherlock Holmes* (London: Mayflower Paperbacks, 1970).

4   "J. Watson" [L. Townsend], *The Sexual Adventures of Sherlock Holmes* (New York: Olympia Press, 1971).

5   R. Stout, "Watson was a Woman," 3–4, 16.

6   V.P. Johnson, "The Adventure of the Misguided Males," *Baker Street Journal,* old ser., 3.4 (1948): 501–505.

7   Examples are: J. Wolff, "That Was No Lady,"*American Journal of Surgery*, 58.2 (1942): 310–12; E. Queen, "High Sherloctane: or, Having Fun With Words," in *In the Queen's Parlour, and Other Leaves from the Editors' Notebook* (New York: Simon & Schuster, 1957), 169–70; and K. Karlson, "Why Watson Wasn't a Woman," *Baker Street Pages*, new ser., 1.2 (1971): 2.

8   Redmond, *In Bed With Sherlock Holmes*, 128.

9   Redmond, *In Bed With Sherlock Holmes*, 43.

10   Redmond, *In Bed With Sherlock Holmes*, 45.

11   Redmond, *In Bed With Sherlock Holmes*, 90.

12   Redmond, *In Bed With Sherlock Holmes*, 91.

13   Redmond, *In Bed With Sherlock Holmes*, 91.

14   DYIN (I, 439)

15   Redmond, *In Bed With Sherlock Holmes*, 91.

16   McQueen, *Sherlock Holmes Detected*, 148.

17   McQueen, *Sherlock Holmes Detected,* 97–98.

18   McQueen, *Sherlock Holmes Detected,* 99.

19   McQueen, *Sherlock Holmes Detected,* 99–100.

20   McQueen, *Sherlock Holmes Detected,* 100.

21 C. Morley, quoted by McQueen, p. 100.

22 I. McQueen, *Sherlock Holmes Detected,* 103.

23 G. Brend, *My Dear Holmes. A Study in Sherlock* (London: Allen and Unwin, 1951), 84.

24 TWIS (I, 369)

25 Brend, *My Dear Holmes,* 89.

26 E.g., Baring-Gould, *Sherlock Holmes of Baker Street*; M. Harrison, *I, Sherlock Holmes* (New York: Dutton, 1977); and M. Hardwick, *Sherlock Holmes. My Life and Crimes* (London: Harvill Press, 1984).

27 E.g., S.C. Roberts, "Dr. Watson" in *Holmes & Watson. A Miscellany* (London: Oxford University Press, 1953), 55–92; and M. Hardwick, *The Private Life of Dr. Watson. Being the Personal Reminiscences of John H. Watson, M.D.* (New York: Dutton, 1983).

28 M. Harrison, *In the Footsteps of Sherlock Holmes* (London: Cassell, 1958); *The London of Sherlock Holmes* (Newton Abbot, Devon: David & Charles, 1972); *The World of Sherlock Holmes* (New York: Dutton, 1975); *A Study in Surmise. The Making of Sherlock Holmes* (Bloomington, Ind.: Gaslight Publications, 1984).

29 J.E. Holroyd, *Baker Street Byways: A Book about Sherlock Holmes* (London: Allen & Unwin, 1959), and other contributions.

30 H.C. Potter, "Reflections and Canonical Vehicles; and Something of the Horse," *Baker Street Journal,* new ser., 21.4 (1971): 200–206, and other contributions.

31 S.C. Roberts, *Holmes & Watson. A Miscellany* (London: Oxford University Press, 1953), and other contributions.

32 W. Shepherd, *On the Scent with Sherlock Holmes. Some Old Problems Resolved* (London: Barker, 1978).

Chapter Twelve

1 Brend, *My Dear Holmes,* 16, presents a good case for 1853 instead, we accept the reasoning of Baring-Gould (I, 47).

2 Baring-Gould, *Sherlock Holmes of Baker Street*; however, his reasoning is more sentimental than logical. An alternative date, the 13th, is considered in APPENDIX II.

3 Baring-Gould, *Sherlock Holmes of Baker Street,* 12.

4 Baring-Gould, *Sherlock Holmes of Baker Street,* 13.

5 Émile Jean Horace Vernet (1789–1863) was "a French painter of martial scenes, the last and greatest of several generations of noted artists." See Tracey, *The Encyclopaedia Sherlockiana,* 379. Vernet's sister was Sherlock's grandmother; see GREE (I, 590).

6 NORW (II, 414)

7 Extreme developments of possible conundrums are considered in APPENDIX II.

8   E.G. Withycombe, *The Oxford Dictionary of English Christian Names*, 2nd ed., (Oxford: Clarendon Press, 1950), 254.

9   M. Cadogan and P. Craig, *You're a Brick, Angela! A New Look at Girl's Fiction from 1839 to 1975* (London: Gollancz, 1976), 15–17.

10   Shakespeare, for example, is quoted several times: e.g. in EMPT (II, 340, 342); LADY (II, 665); and ABBE (II, 491).

11   EMPT (II, 336–37)

12   D.L. Sayers, "Holmes's College Career," 1–34; O.F. Grazebrook, *Oxford or Cambridge?* (London: privately printed, 1949); and Brend, *My Dear Holmes*, 18–28.

13   STUD (I, 148)

14   STUD (I, 150)

15   STUD (I, 153)

16   STUD (I, 154)

17   STUD (I, 161)

18   STUD (I, 162–63)

19   STUD (I, 254)

20   SPEC (I, 252)

21   GLOR (I, 108)

22   REIG (I, 330)

23   VALL (I, 510)

24   SIGN (I, 611)

25   SIGN (I, 612)

26   SIGN (I, 613)

27   SCAN (I, 347–48)

28   BOSC (II, 134); see also 38–39 herein.

29   FIVE (I, 395)

30   COPP (II, 115); see also 47–48 herein.

31   DYIN (I, 439); see also 49–50 herein.

32   FINA (II, 304)

33   FINA (II, 305)

34   EMPT (II, 347)

35   FINA (II, 302): as Baring-Gould (II, 307) points out, this reference to Mortimer Street is "a little mysterious, to say the least: it would not seem to fit in with either of Watson's earlier-mentioned practices, that in Kensington or that in Paddington, since Mortimer Street runs parallel to Oxford Street and is not in either district." We believe we are presenting the correct interpretation of the Watsons' changing circumstances.

36   FINA (II, 302)

37   FINA (II, 307)

38   FINA (II, 307–8)

39   FINA (II, 309)

40   FINA (II, 310)

41   FINA (II, 310)

42   FINA (II, 311)

43   FINA (II, 312)

44   FINA (II, 312)

45   FINA (II, 314–17); EMPT (II, 333–36)

46   EMPT (II, 333–36)

47   EMPT (II, 348)

48   EMPT (II, 342–43); see also 57 herein.

49   LAST (II, 801)

50   EMPT (II, 345)

51   EMPT (II, 333)

52   NORW (II, 414)

53   LADY (II, 661); see also 73–74 herein.

54   CHAS (II, 563–64); see also 76–77 herein.

55   HOUN (II, 83–84); see also 77 and 80–83 herein.

56   3GAR (II, 653–54); see also 87–89 herein.

57   ILLU (II, 672); see also 90–92 herein.

58   BLAN (II, 707); see also 93–96 herein.

59   Her attractions are made clear partly through Watson's description (TWIS, II, 378) and partly because of the care that Sherlock took to leave before Mrs. St. Clair rose (II, 382), so as to ensure Watson was removed swiftly from them!

60   See 92–93 herein.

61   3GAB (II, 733–34); see also 96–100 herein.

62   3GAB (II, 728–29); see also 96–100 herein.

63   MAZA (II, 735)

64   CREE (II, 761–72): see also 104–7 herein.

65   CREE (II, 760): see also 104–7 herein.

66   She was persuaded, not only by the British foreign Minister, Sir Edward Grey, but by Prime Minister Herbert Asquith himself; see LAST (II, 801).

67   Yet it might just be worth searching the parish records for mention of the burial of Charlotte Holmes—or was it, by then, Charlotte Watson?

Appendix I

1   H.W. Bell, *Sherlock Holmes and Dr. Watson: the Chronology of their Adventures* (London: Constable, 1932).

2   Brend, *My Dear Holmes.*

3   W.S. Baring-Gould, *The Annotated Sherlock Holmes*, 2 vols, (New York: Potter, 1967).

4   Dakin, *A Sherlock Holmes Commentary.*

5   "The Resident Patient." *Strand Magazine*, 6.32 (Aug. 1893): 128–38: quoted also in RESI (I, 267).

6   *Strand Magazine.*

7   *Strand Magazine.*

8   BERY (II, 282)

9   E.B. Zeisler, *Baker Street Chronology: Commentaries on the Sacred Writings of Dr. John H. Watson* (Chicago: Isaacs, 1953), 68–69.

10 D.M. Dakin, 88.

11 NOBL (I, 281)

12 NOBL (I, 282)

13 NOBL (I, 282)

14 D.M. Dakin, 84.

15 FIVE (I, 389)

16 FIVE (I, 396)

17 FIVE (I, 399)

18 FIVE (I, 392)

19 FIVE (I, 390)

20 Zeisler, *Baker Street Chronology*, 78–79.

21 J.F. Christ, *An Irregular Chronology of Sherlock Holmes of Baker Street* (Chicago: The Fanlight House, 1947), 13.

22 TWIS (I, 368)

23 D.M. Dakin, 72.

24 SCAN (I, 347)

25 SCAN (I, 346)

26 FIVE (I, 389)

27 ENGI (II, 209)

28 CROO (II, 225)

29 ENGI (II, 221)

30 D.M. Dakin, 119.

31 IDEN (I, 404)

32 IDEN (I, 412)

33 IDEN (I, 405)

34 IDEN (I, 404)

35 Dakin, *A Sherlock Holmes Commentary*, 49.

36 REDH (I, 418)

37 DYIN (I, 440)

38 Dakin, *A Sherlock Holmes Commentary*, 162.

39 WIST (II, 238)

40 Dakin, *A Sherlock Holmes Commentary*, 218.

41 WIST (II, 242)

42   Dakin, *A Sherlock Holmes Commentary*, 237.

43   HOUN (II, 5)

44   Brend, *My Dear Holmes*, 100.

45   CARD (II, 193)

46   COPP (II, 115)

47   COPP (II, 115)

48   COPP (II, 115)

49   Brend, *My Dear Holmes*, 180.

50   DANC (II, 529)

51   RETI (II, 546)

52   RETI (II, 547)

53   DANC (II, 531)

54   Brend, *My Dear Holmes*, 180.

55   RETI (II, 548)

APPENDIX III

1   H. Still, *Of Time, Tides, and Inner Clocks* (Harrisburg, Pa.: Stackpole, 1972), 47–48.

2   G.L. Playfair and S. Hill, *The Cycles of Heaven* (London: Pan Books, 1978), 217–29.

3   Playfair and Hill, *The Cycles of Heaven*, 217–29.

4   Playfair and Hill, *The Cycles of Heaven*, 217–29.

5   REIG (I, 331)

6   REIG (I, 331)

7   REIG (I, 331)

8   VALL (I, 471)

9   N.L. Bengis, "What was the Month?" *Baker Street Journal*, new ser., 7.4 (1957): 204–14.

$\mathcal{B}ibliography$

Baring-Gould, William S. *The Annotated Sherlock Holmes*. 2 vols. New York: Potter, 1967.

————. *Sherlock Holmes of Baker Street. A Biography of the World's First Consulting Detective*. London: Hart-Davis, 1962.

Bell, Harold W. *Sherlock Holmes and Dr. Watson: the Chronology of their Adventures*. London: Constable, 1932.

Bengis, Nathan L. "Sherlock Stays after School." *The Illustrious Clients' Second Case-Book*. Ed. J.N. Williamson. Indianapolis: The Illustrious Clients, 1949.

————. "What was the Month?" *Baker Street Journal*, new ser., 7.4 (1957): 204–14.

Boucher, Anthony. "Was the Later Holmes an Imposter?" *Profile by Gaslight*. Ed. E.W. Smith. New York: Simon and Schuster, 1944.

Bradley, C. Alan & William A.S. Sarjeant. "The Woman." *From the Mantelpiece* 4.4 (1979).

Brend, Gavin. *My Dear Holmes. A Study In Sherlock*. London: Allen and Unwin, 1951.

Cadogan, Mary & Patricia Craig. *You're a Brick, Angela! A New Look at Girl's Fiction from 1839 to 1975*. London: Gollancz, 1976.

Christ, Jay Finley. *An Irregular Chronology of Sherlock Holmes of Baker Street*. Chicago: The Fanlight House, 1947.

Dakin, D. Martin. *A Sherlock Holmes Commentary*. Newton Abbot, Devon: David & Charles, 1972.

Davies, Bernard. "Holmes and the Halls." *Sherlock Holmes Journal* 7.3 (1965): 68–73.

Davies, Colin. "A Scandal in Baker Street." *The Guardian* 30 March 1974. [Also publ. in *Sherlockiana* 19.2–3 (1974): 10–11; *Sherlock Holmes Journal* 11.4 (1974): 124–26]

De Waal, Ronald B. *The International Sherlock Holmes*. Hamden, Conn.: Archon
Books, 1980.

———. *The World Bibliography of Sherlock Holmes and Dr. Watson. A Classified and
Annotated List of Materials Relating to their Lives and Adventures*. New York: Bramhall
House, 1974.

Grazebrook, Owen F. *Oxford or Cambridge?* London: privately printed, 1949.

Hardwick, Michael. *The Private Life of Dr. Watson. Being the Personal Reminiscences of
John H. Watson, M.D.* New York: Dutton, 1983.

———. *Sherlock Holmes. My Life and Crimes*. London: Harvill Press, 1984.

Hardwick, Michael & Mollie Hardwick. *The Private Life of Sherlock Holmes*.
London: Mayflower Paperbacks, 1970.

Harrison, Michael. *In the Footsteps of Sherlock Holmes*. London: Cassell, 1958.

———. *The London of Sherlock Holmes*. Newton Abbot, Devon: David &
Charles, 1972.

———. *I, Sherlock Holmes*. New York: Dutton, 1977.

———. *A Study in Surmise. The Making of Sherlock Holmes*. Bloomington, Ind.: Gaslight
Publications, 1984.

———. *The World of Sherlock Holmes*. New York: Dutton, 1975.

Heldenbrand, Page. "The Duplicity of Sherlock Holmes." *Two Baker Street
Akronisms*. Summit, New Jersey: The Pamphlet House, 1945.

Henderson, David. "No Sich Person." *Sherlock Holmes Journal* 7.3 (1965): 93–94.

Holroyd, James Edward. *Baker Street Byways: A Book about Sherlock Holmes*.
London: Allen & Unwin, 1959.

———. "The Egg Spoon." *Sherlock Holmes Journal* 1.1 (1952): 24–26.

Howell, M. & P. Ford. *The True History of the Elephant Man*. New York: Allison &
Busby, 1980.

Johnson, Virginia P. "The Adventure of the Misguided Males." *Baker Street Journal*, old
ser. 3.4 (1948): 501–5.

Karlson, Katherine. "Why Watson Wasn't a Woman." *Baker Street Pages*, new ser. 1.2
(1971): 2.

Katz, Robert S. "Mary Morstan Moriarty." *Baker Street Journal*, new ser. 27.1 (1977): 22–23.

Kennedy, Bruce D. "Cherchez La Femme." *A Curious Collection*. Ed. W. J. Walsh. Suffern,
N.Y.: The Musgrave Ritualists Beta, 1971.

———. "The Truth about Nero Wolfe." *Baker Street Journal*, old ser. 18.3 (1967): 154–55.

Leavitt, Robert Keith. "Annie Oakley in Baker Street." *Profile by Gaslight*. Ed. E.W. Smith.
New York: Simon & Schuster, 1944.

McMillan, S. and James, G. "The Guns of Sherlock Holmes." *Guns & Ammo* (April
1975): 50–53, 83.

McQueen, Ian. *Sherlock Holmes Detected*. Newton Abbot: David & Charles, 1974.

Meaker, S. R. "Watson Medicus." *The Third Cab*. Boston, Mass.: The Speckled
Band, 1960.

Meyer, Nicholas. *The Seven-Per-Cent Solution. Being a Reprint from the Reminiscences of John H. Watson, M. D.* New York: Dutton, 1974.

Nakagawa, Yuro. *Holmes wa onna datta.* Tokyo: Hayakawa Shobo, 1980.

Pearson, R. "A Scandal in Kent." *Serpentine Muse* 6.1 (1981): 4–12.

Playfair, Giles. "John and James." *Baker Street Journal*, new ser. 5.2 (1946): 121.

Playfair, Guy L. and S. Hill. *The Cycles of Heaven.* London: Pan Books, 1978.

Potter, Henry C. "The Case of the Blatant Duplication." *Baker Street Journal*, new ser. 20.2 (1970): 36–90.

———. "Reflections and Canonical Vehicles; and something of the Horse." *Baker Street Journal*, new ser. 21.4 (1971): 200–206.

———. "The Veiled Lodger Revisited." *Baker Street Journal*, new ser. 22.3 (1972): 158–65.

Queen, Ellery. "High Sherloctane: or, Having Fun With Words." *In the Queen's Parlor, and Other Leaves from the Editors' Notebook.* New York: Simon & Schuster, 1957.

Redmond, Christopher. *In Bed with Sherlock Holmes.* Toronto: Simon & Pierre, 1984.

Roberts, Sydney C. "Dr. Watson." *Holmes and Watson. A Miscellany.* London: Oxford University Press, 1953.

———. *Dr. Watson: Prolegomena to the Study of a Biographical Problem, with a Bibliography of Sherlock Holmes.* London: Faber & Faber, 1931.

Sayers, Dorothy L. "Dr. Watson's Christian Name." *Profile by Gaslight.* Ed. E.W. Smith. New York: Simon & Schuster, 1944.

———. "Holmes's College Career." *Baker Street Studies.* Ed. H.W. Bell. London: Constable, 1934.

Shepherd, Walter. *On the Scent with Sherlock Holmes. Some Old Problems Resolved.* London: Barker, 1978.

Simpson, A. Carson. "It Must Have Been Two Other Fellows." *Leaves from the Copper Beeches.* Narberth, Pa.: Livingston Publishing Co., 1959.

Sims, G. R., ed. *Living London.* London: Cassell, 1901.

Sorkin, Esther. "Heresy." *Sherlockian Meddler* 7.4 (1979): 30–32.

Starrett, Vincent. *The Private Life of Sherlock Holmes.* Rev. ed. London: Allen and Unwin, 1960.

Still, H. *Of Time, Tides, and Inner Clocks.* Harrisburg, Pa.: Stackpole, 1972.

Stout, Rex. "Watson Was a Woman." *Saturday Review of Literature* 23.19 (1941): 3–4, 16.

Strand Magazine 1–70 (1893–1927).

Tracey, Jack. *The Encyclopaedia Sherlockiana; or, A Universal Dictionary of the State of Knowledge of Sherlock Holmes and his Biographer John H. Watson, M.D.* New York: Doubleday, 1977.

"Watson, John H." [L. Townsend]. *The Sexual Adventures of Sherlock Holmes.* New York: Olympia Press, 1971.

Withycombe, E. G. *The Oxford Dictionary of English Christian Names.* 2nd ed. Oxford: Clarendon Press, 1950.

Wolff, Julian. "That Was No Lady." *American Journal of Surgery* 58.2 (1942): 310-12.

Zeisler, Ernest B. *Baker Street Chronology: Commentaries on the Sacred Writings of Dr. John H. Watson.* Chicago: Isaacs, 1953.

Index

Alan Bradley

C. Alan Bradley grew up in Cobourg, Ontario. He completed his electronics education in Peterborough, and majored in Television Engineering and Communications with CREI (Washington, D.C.).

After a jack-of-all-trades stint at home-town radio station CHUC, in Cobourg, he went on to CKTB, St. Catharines, CJSS-TV, Cornwall, and became Chief Engineer of CHOV-TV in Pembroke. After a time in the television studios of the (then) Ryerson Polytechnical Institute, in Toronto, he moved West to take up a position as Director of Television Engineering at the University of Saskatchewan's Instructional Media Centre, where he became a pioneer in the broadcasting of satellite (Distance Education) classes, and taught script-writing and television production classes through the University's Extension Division.

After twenty-five years he retired from the University of Saskatchewan to devote himself to writing screenplays. He has optioned an action/adventure drama to Hollywood; his scripts have gained recognition in national and international workshops, and have received praise from industry giants such as Francis Ford Coppola's American Zoetrope Company. His writings have appeared in *The Globe and Mail*, *The National Post*, *Grain*, and elsewhere, and have been broadcast on CBC Radio. He lives in Kelowna, British Columbia with his wife, Shirley, and two calculating cats. He is presently at work on a detective novel while waiting for an opportunity to adapt *Ms. Holmes of Baker Street* to the big screen.

William A.S. Sarjeant

William Antony Swithin Sarjeant, geologist, folksinger, book collector, fantasy writer and Sherlockian scholar, was born in Sheffield, England on St. Swithin's Day, July 15th 1935. In 1972, after a number of years on the faculty of the Geology Department at the University of Nottingham, he, his wife, Peggy, and young family, immigrated to Saskatoon, Canada, where he took up a faculty position in the Department of Geological Sciences at the University of Saskatchewan, a position he held until his passing.

In his spare time, Bill performed with a local folk group called the Prairie Higglers and wrote a series of fantasy novels under the pen name, Antony Swithin. He was deeply interested in Sherlockian matters and in detective fiction in general. Along with Alan Bradley, he was a founding member of the Casebook of Saskatoon, one of Canada's oldest Sherlockian societies. In 1986, he was elected a Master Bootmaker of Toronto. He published many articles on detective fiction in *The Armchair Detective, Canadian Holmes, The Mystery Fancier* and *The Poisoned Pen*. During the last months of his life, Bill was in the midst of writing a series of articles on crime writers as authors of children's fiction. He died in Saskatoon on July 8th 2002.